WARFARE
in the
MEDIEVAL WORLD

HISTORY OF WARFARE

Chris Marshall

RSVP

**RAINTREE
STECK-VAUGHN**
PUBLISHERS
A Steck-Vaughn Company

Steck-Vaughn Company

First published 1999 by Raintree Steck-Vaughn Publishers,
an imprint of Steck-Vaughn Company.
Copyright © 1999 Brown Partworks Limited.

Library of Congress Cataloging-in-Publication Data

Marshall, Chris, 1962–
    Warfare in the Medieval world / Chris Marshall.
        p.   cm. — (History of warfare)
    Includes bibliographical references and index.
    Summary: Provides an overview of the evolution of military conflicts from the fifth through the fifteenth centuries, describing changes in the make-up of the armies, fighting tactics, and weapons.
        ISBN 0-8172-5443-9
        1. Military art and science — History — Juvenile literature.
    2. Military history, Medieval — Juvenile literature.   [1. Military history, Medieval.   2.Military art and science — History.]   I. Title.
    II. Series; History of Warfare (Austin, Tex.)
    U37.M37   1999
    355'.009'02 — dc21

98-11957
CIP
AC

Printed and bound in the United States
1 2 3 4 5 6 7 8 9 0 IP 03 02 01 00 99 98

Brown Partworks Limited
Managing Editor: Ian Westwell
Senior Designer: Paul Griffin
Picture Researcher: Wendy Verren
Editorial Assistant: Antony Shaw
Cartographers: William le Bihan, John See
Index: Pat Coward

Raintree Steck-Vaughn
Publishing Director: Walter Kossmann
Project Manager: Joyce Spicer
Editor: Shirley Shalit

Front cover: The Burgundian attack on the town of Grandson, Switzerland, in 1476 (main picture) and the Norman leader Robert Guiscard (inset).
Page 1: The Crusaders reach Jerusalem, 1099.

Consultant
Dr. Niall Barr, Senior Lecturer,
Royal Military Academy Sandhurst,
Camberley, Surrey, England

Acknowledgments listed on page 80 constitute part of this copyright page.

CONTENTS

INTRODUCTION

This volume looks at the history of war between the 5th and late 15th centuries. For most of this period both wars and campaigns were decided by a single, decisive battle. Most countries did not have the wealth to support a large permanent army in times of peace or fight long wars. Most noblemen were obliged to follow their ruler to war for a set period—three months, for example—and were then free to head for home.

The core of a medieval army was made up of mounted warriors, chiefly lance-armed armored knights. Although few in number, knights and their personal followers, known as men-at-arms, were the dominant force on the battlefield. A single thunderous charge often decided a battle. Knights were highly trained and carried better weapons than the humble infantrymen who made up the bulk of any army.

However, as the medieval period drew to a close the foot soldier began to overtake the cavalryman in importance. Archers, particularly those armed with the longbow, had the hitting power to stop a cavalry charge in its tracks, while pikemen with their long spears proved they could take on and defeat cavalry in hand-to-hand combat. Infantrymen were especially successful against knights, if they fought behind defenses such as ditches.

Toward the end of the period gunpowder weapons—primitive firearms and cannon—were also being used in battles and sieges, and the first professional standing armies were being formed.

Commanders in the medieval world held their position because they were rulers or nobles, not because they were trained generals in the modern sense. Most were competent, although a few were outstanding.

Many commanders saw their job as seeking out the enemy as quickly as possible and then leading by example, fighting bravely in the front rank. Once a battle began, they often had little impact on its development. At the end of the medieval era commanders were beginning to stand back from the confused fighting. From this vantage point they could direct their forces with greater control.

Castles and fortified towns played an important role in medieval warfare until the arrival of cannon. Castles were used to protect a vulnerable area from attack, to control a rebellious region, or were a base from which an army could launch an offensive. Sieges were time-consuming and costly, and more castles fell to treachery, disease, and hunger than assault. The introduction of cannon, however, sounded the death knell of castles because artillery could smash stone walls with ease.

War in the medieval world was neither stagnant nor unchanging. New weapons were introduced, and armies became increasingly professional. By the end of the 15th century, war was no longer a contest solely between nobles but was becoming a conflict between armies of trained soldiers, the vast majority drawn from outside the ranks of the nobility.

THE EARLY BYZANTINE EMPIRE

In the second half of the 5th century A.D. the Roman Empire still existed but had split. The western half was controlled from Italy, while the eastern half was ruled from Constantinople (Istanbul in modern Turkey). Hostile tribes, called barbarians by the Romans, had broken through the empire's borders. The barbarians brought the western empire to an end in 476. The eastern empire was threatened by many enemies, but it survived for 1,000 years. Historians call this part of the former Roman Empire the Byzantine Empire.

Constantinople was the heart of the Byzantine Empire. From there a succession of mighty emperors ruled over a great kingdom. Its capture, after a siege by the Ottoman Turks in 1453, marked the end of the 1,000-year-old empire.

Justinian I (fifth from right) ruled the Byzantine Empire from 527 to 565 and proved to be an energetic emperor. His armies were led by two of the most able generals of the age, Belisarius and Narses, and restored the empire's former borders.

The Byzantine Empire is so-called because the city of Constantinople, its capital, was previously called Byzantium. Its name was changed in A.D. 330 to honor the Roman emperor Constantine I. In the late 5th century A.D. the empire stretched from what are now the Balkans in the west, across Turkey, and into the Middle East. It also included Egypt and parts of Libya. At the eastern edge of the large empire lay the border with Byzantium's great rival, Persia.

Persian expansion into Byzantium

Conflict between the empire and Persia had been going on for hundreds of years. In 502 the two began a series of wars that lasted on and off for 100 years. One cause of the wars was Persian expansion into Byzantine territory. Another was the religious differences between the Christian Byzantines and the non-Christian Persians. There was also a quarrel over who was to pay for their joint defense against fierce nomads—the Huns. These deadly enemies were trying to break into the region from the north.

BELISARIUS

The Byzantine military genius Belisarius rose to fame through his exploits in Emperor Justinian's First Persian War (524–532). He also helped to put down a serious rebellion against Justinian in Constantinople soon afterward.

Belisarius went on to serve Justinian faithfully throughout his career. The emperor, though, seems to have been jealous of his general's success and did not trust him. Justinian ordered him back to Constantinople from North Africa in 544, so that he could keep a close watch on him for signs of treason.

Despite this jealousy Justinian always turned to Belisarius whenever the going got tough. In 554 the emperor called him out of retirement to take charge of a Byzantine campaign in southern Spain. Five years after that, with barbarian invaders almost at the gates of Constantinople, Justinian once again recalled Belisarius. The general saved the imperial capital from the invaders. After these heroics Belisarius returned to retirement. But Justinian accused him of treason and put him in prison in 562.

The following year the emperor decided that he had been wrong. Belisarius was released to live the rest of his life in peace.

Belisarius pictured as an old man after years of successful campaigns to expand the frontiers of the Byzantine Empire.

The First Persian War (524–532) was fought during the reign of Emperor Justinian I. Justinian launched the career of Belisarius. Belisarius was one of the most brilliant Byzantine generals. In 530, heavily outnumbered, he defeated the Persians at the Battle of Dara. He goaded the 40,000-strong Persian army into assaulting his foot soldiers, whom he put behind trenches. As the Persians advanced into the trap, the Byzantine cavalry fanned out to the left and right. Then the Byzantine armored cavalry—the cataphracts—surrounded the Persians, launched a superb charge, and destroyed them.

Battle against the barbarians

When that First Persian War ended, Justinian decided to regain the old western empire from the barbarians. He chose Belisarius to lead the campaign. Belisarius struck first at North Africa, which was then ruled by a German barbarian tribe called the Vandals. The Vandals had spread across Northern Europe into Spain and crossed over to North Africa in the 5th century A.D.

A Byzantine fleet landed in what is now Tunisia in September 533. Some 15,000 men poured off the ships and marched on the ancient city of Carthage, the Vandals' capital. They met no resistance until they were near the city. At this point three forces commanded by the Vandal king, Gelimer, attacked the Byzantine invaders as they moved into a narrow valley ten miles (16 km) from Carthage.

The Vandals' timing was poor. Instead of attacking together at the front, center, and rear of Belisarius's army, they struck in three separate waves. Belisarius and his troops were able to deal with each Vandal force in turn. Many of his troops were Hun cavalry, mounted warriors much feared for their lightning attacks and devastating archery. After this Battle of Ad Decimum the Byzantines marched unopposed into the capital. The defeated barbarian forces fled into the desert.

The following December though, the Vandals were back with a large army, including local tribesmen. Belisarius took his army to confront the Vandals at Tricameron, 30 miles (48 km) from the capital. Immediately Belisarius launched a

CATAPHRACT CAVALRY

Byzantine cataphracts were heavy cavalry dressed in armor from head to foot. The term cataphract comes from the Greek word for "covered"–both the horse and the rider were covered with metal armor.

This type of heavy cavalry first appeared in the armies of the Parthian Empire, which existed in Asia during the time of the Romans. The Romans fought many wars against the Parthians. The Romans were impressed with the cataphracts and created heavy cavalry units of their own. The Byzantines later made the cataphracts the major force in their army.

Mounted on powerful warhorses, Byzantine cataphract cavalrymen bristled with weapons. They usually carried a bow, a lance, a sword, and a dagger. Besides body armor they wore an iron helmet and carried a shield. The shield was strapped to the arm so they could use both hands to control their horses. The main cataphract tactic was "shock action," a ferocious charge that crashed through any enemy.

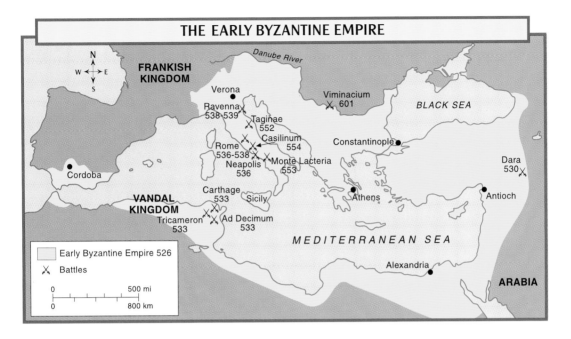

THE EARLY BYZANTINE EMPIRE

Early Byzantine Empire 526

X Battles

0 — 500 mi
0 — 800 km

series of cavalry charges against a force that outnumbered his troops by almost ten-to-one. The Byzantines drove the Vandals back. At this point Belisarius's Hun horsemen, mercenaries whose loyalty to the Byzantine Empire was doubtful, decided they were on the winning side and charged. The Vandals ran.

War against the Ostrogoths

The Vandal kingdom in North Africa was finished, but it took until 548 for the Byzantines to complete their conquest of the local tribes. Justinian recalled Belisarius almost immediately after Tricameron and sent him to invade Italy. Italy was ruled by the Ostrogoths, another barbarian tribe. Belisarius began his campaign by invading the island of Sicily in 535. He easily conquered the island and then laid siege to the important city of Naples (then known as Neapolis) on the Italian mainland.

After about three weeks of blockade one of the Byzantine soldiers discovered a disused waterway leading into the city, which allowed Belisarius to smuggle a force under the city walls. A simultaneous attack by these troops and the besiegers outside ended in a complete Byzantine victory. Belisarius's forces, which contained many barbarian troops, then showed what happened to people who resisted them. The Byzantines rampaged through Naples, burning, looting, and killing at will.

The Byzantine Empire spread through much of the Mediterranean thanks to the major victories of Belisarius and Narses.

9

Ostrogoth besiegers try to storm the walls of Rome in 537. Belisarius, although outnumbered, was able to prevent the city from being captured. The Ostrogoths were forced to retreat when a Byzantine relief force arrived the next year.

Rome was Belisarius's next target. He arrived there in December 536 to find the city undefended. The Ostrogoths had decided they needed time to build up their forces and had withdrawn to Ravenna, a port on the east coast. The following March the Ostrogoths returned and surrounded Rome. They cut off its water supply and began a blockade. The siege dragged on. The Ostrogoths could not break in—Rome's walls and Belisarius's catapults and ballistas (arrow-firing catapults) saw to that. But the Byzantines could not break out. Eventually Byzantine reinforcements arrived and the Ostrogoths withdrew in 538.

Belisarius chased the Ostrogoths back to Ravenna and besieged them. With no other choice the Ostrogoths offered to make Belisarius their king if he turned against Constantinople.

When Belisarius seemed to agree, the Ostrogoths opened the gates of Ravenna. Once inside, though, Belisarius captured the Ostrogoth leaders and led them back to Constantinople as his prisoners. Belisarius was not allowed to rest, however. Another war with Persia had started, and he was needed in the east.

Narses in Italy

The Ostrogoths, however, were not finished in Italy. As soon as Belisarius had left, they broke out of their remaining strongholds and took back most of the territory the Byzantines had captured. Belisarius returned in 544 but was not given a big enough army to regain the lost territory. Justinian had to send another general, Narses, this time with a force of 20,000 to 35,000 men. The elderly Narses was not a trained soldier. He was an official at the Byzantine court, but he proved to be a great general.

Marching into Italy from the north in 552, Narses quickly crushed the Ostrogoths at the Battle of Taginae in June. His soldiers killed the Ostrogoth leader, Totila, and more than 6,000 of his troops. Narses then continued south and captured Rome for the empire once again. The Ostrogoths headed farther south to Naples. Narses followed and defeated the Ostrogoth army completely at the Battle of Monte Lacteria (553).

NARSES AND THE BATTLE OF TAGINAE

In June 552 the Byzantine army came face to face with an Ostrogoth force in a narrow valley at Taginae in Italy. The Byzantines were commanded by the elderly Narses. He knew little of military matters but he made the right decisions against the Ostrogoths.

Narses arranged his men in a semicircle. In the center he placed foot soldiers armed with short spears and shields. To each side of them he fanned out cataphract armored cavalry and foot archers. Narses also put a group of archers high up on one side of the valley.

As the 15,000 Ostrogoths came into bow range, the Byzantine archers on the ridge opened fire. Then the Byzantine cataphracts and foot archers stationed on the valley floor joined in. Their arrows stopped the barbarian advance.

Narses then moved in for the kill. While the foot archers kept the Ostrogoths busy, the Byzantine cataphracts encircled the confused and disorganized barbarian forces and destroyed them. More than 6,000 Ostrogoths were killed and those left fled for their lives. Narses then moved on to take Rome.

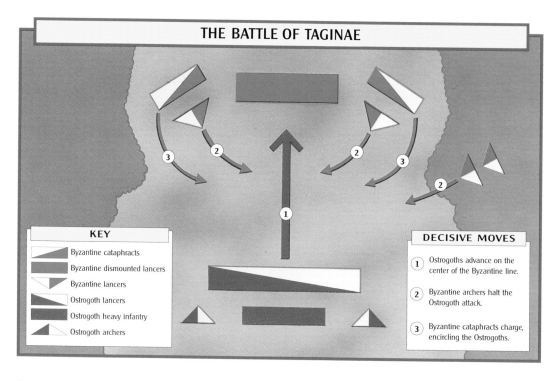

THE BATTLE OF TAGINAE

KEY

- Byzantine cataphracts
- Byzantine dismounted lancers
- Byzantine lancers
- Ostrogoth lancers
- Ostrogoth heavy infantry
- Ostrogoth archers

DECISIVE MOVES

1. Ostrogoths advance on the center of the Byzantine line.
2. Byzantine archers halt the Ostrogoth attack.
3. Byzantine cataphracts charge, encircling the Ostrogoths.

Fought in Italy during 552, the Battle of Taginae was one of the Byzantine Empire's greatest victories over the barbarians who were attempting to keep their stranglehold on the country.

Narses's task in Italy was not over, though. Another barbarian army invaded Italy. This time it was the Franks, who poured over the Alps from the north. In the spring of 554 the Frankish and Byzantine forces met at Casilinum. Narses, outnumbered nearly two-to-one, took up a defensive position. His forces spread out in a semicircle and waited for the Franks to advance.

As the solid mass of barbarians marched toward the Byzantines, Narses's archers opened fire on them from the left and right. Meanwhile the Byzantine cavalry surrounded the Franks and then rode at them in a thunderous charge. Narses won the battle. Italy was again part of the Byzantine Empire.

A new barbarian threat

While Belisarius and Narses were conquering Italy, taking it away from the Ostrogoths and Franks, other barbarian peoples were threatening the Byzantine Empire's borders. Nomadic tribes were pouring out of Asia into Europe. They forced people in their path to move out or be destroyed. The Bulgars and the Slavs found themselves in the way of the Asian nomads in about 530. In order to escape, both peoples tried to invade the Balkan area of the Byzantine Empire.

To protect the empire from these raids, the Byzantines hired a third group of barbarians, the Avars. However, the Avars, who were skilled horse-mounted archers, began to create an empire of their own in the region. In 568 they drove the Lombard people out of their homelands along the Danube River. They fled into Italy. The Lombards in turn conquered all the Byzantine territory there except for a few areas in the south. Then the Avars began to strike at the Byzantine Empire in the Balkans. In the end the Byzantine emperor Maurice went to war and defeated the Avars at the Battle of Viminacium in 601.

Maurice was a skilled general. Besides his success in halting the Avars in the Balkans, he had also ended the war with Persia by winning a key battle against them in 591. However, Maurice's strict discipline led to a military rebellion in 602 and his own execution. The Avars and the Persians wasted no time in attacking the Byzantine Empire again. Another force—Islam—would also soon threaten Byzantine territories in the Middle East.

Byzantine troops led by Narses battle against the Ostrogoths at Monte Lacteria in 553. The Ostrogoths were crushed and their king, Teias, killed in this very heavily one-sided battle.

THE ISLAMIC EMPIRE

In A.D. 622 the religion of Islam was founded by the prophet Mohammed in the Arab city of Medina (now in modern Saudi Arabia). Within ten years his followers, known as Muslims, had spread Islam over all Arabia. The Muslims then launched a devastating military campaign. Their wars took Islam to every corner of the Middle East and into the wider world beyond. The Muslims swept through the southern Mediterranean and the Middle East and also established control over much of the Spanish Peninsula.

The prophet Mohammed (top right) was the founder of the Islamic religion in A.D. 622.

The first to feel the force of the Muslim armies were the two great empires of Byzantium and Persia. In 633 Muslim forces struck blows against both. Their armies swept east into Persian Mesopotamia (modern Iraq) and west into Byzantine Syria. The two empires were exhausted after years of war against one another. It did not take long for the Muslims to win victories over their weaker enemies.

In Syria the Muslims defeated the Byzantines at the Battle of the Yarmuk River (636). The Muslim victory was aided by a mutiny in the Byzantine army before the battle. The Muslims went on to capture the region's major cities, including Jerusalem. They also attacked Egypt, capturing Alexandria in 642. In Mesopotamia the Muslims beat the Persians at the Battles of the Qadasiya River and Jalula (637). By 650 they ruled Persia.

Into North Africa

The Muslims also extended their empire westward. They had attacked North Africa in 642, immediately after their invasion of Egypt, and soon made further gains. The conquest of Libya came quickly. However, the Muslims then tried to push farther west along the North Africa coast but they met fierce resistance from the Berber tribesmen who lived there. It took until

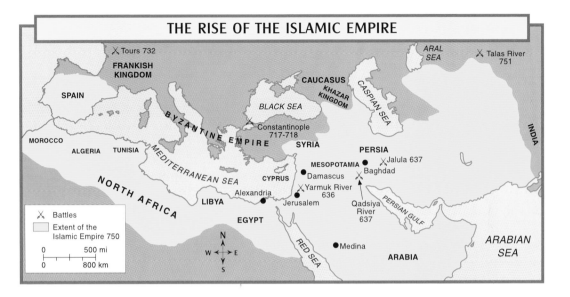

THE RISE OF THE ISLAMIC EMPIRE

705 for the Muslims to conquer the large area that is now divided between Tunisia, Algeria, and Morocco. Six years later they invaded Spain, bringing Islam to Western Europe.

By 715 the Muslim Empire extended from Spain in the west, eastward into Central Asia. In 727 the Muslims went to war with the Khazars, whose kingdom bordered their own to the north. The Muslims succeeded in pushing the Khazar frontier back to the Caucasus, the area between the Black and Caspian Seas.

The extent of the Muslim Empire at the height of its power during the middle of the 8th century.

Muslim expansion halted

While this struggle was taking place, Muslim armies in Central Asia were fighting the Chinese and Turks. In 751 the Muslims defeated the Chinese at the Battle of the Talas River. This victory extended their empire to the borders of China itself. But the Muslims met setbacks. The Byzantines withstood a Muslim siege of Constantinople in 717–718. At the Battle of Tours in 732 the Franks repelled a Muslim invasion of southwest France.

There was also a split in the Muslim world. In 750 a rebellion overthrew the Omayyad ruling house, which withdrew from the Syrian city of Damascus, the capital of the empire, to rule in Spain. A new dynasty—the Abbasids—established itself at Baghdad (now in modern Iraq) and took control of the main empire. The empire was no longer united. Though some conquests were still to be made, the great days of Muslim military expansion had come to an end.

THE CAROLINGIAN EMPIRE

When the Roman Empire in the west came to an end in A.D. 476, several barbarian states took its place. The most powerful of these was known as the kingdom of the Franks. By the close of the 6th century the Frankish kingdom covered a large area of Western Europe. It included modern Belgium, most of France, and parts of Germany. The main kingdom consisted of four regions—Austrasia, Neustria, Burgundy, and Aquitaine. However, the leaders of the Franks were continually trying to expand their empire's borders.

The Battle of Tours, was fought by the Franks under Charles Martel against a Muslim invasion force in 732. It was a decisive moment in European history. Martel's victory stopped the spread of Islam, making sure that Europe would remain Christian.

During the 7th century the Frankish royal house, which had governed for more than 100 years, gradually lost its authority. Power passed to strong, independent lords who ended up ruling the kingdom. One of the most important of these was Charles Martel. He rose to power in 714. However, the kingdom was in a state of civil war, and its four regions were divided. By 719 Martel had successfully reunited Austrasia, Neustria, and Burgundy.

Mediterranean foothold

Aquitaine, the fourth region of the Frankish kingdom, was under threat from Muslims raiding across the high Pyrenees Mountains from Spain. In 719 the Muslims captured the city of Narbonne. This victory gave them a foothold on the Frankish side of the mountains.

Muslim military operations increased until Aquitaine could no longer hold out alone. Eudo, the region's ruler, turned for help to Charles Martel. Martel defeated the Muslims at the Battle of Tours in southwestern France (732) and drove them back into their fortified bases along the Mediterranean coast.

The rise of the Carolingians

Charles was succeeded as the most powerful Frankish lord by his son Pepin. In 751 Pepin overthrew the Frankish king, Childeric III, and had himself crowned in his place. In this way Pepin began the dynasty of the Carolingians—the descendants of Charles Martel. Pepin brought Aquitaine back under his control. He also recaptured the coastal region around Narbonne from the Muslims. The Arabs retreated to Spain. When Pepin died in 768, his sons Carloman and Charles ruled the empire. Carloman soon died, but his brother went on to rule until 814. He became known as Charles the Great, or Charlemagne, because of his triumphs.

THE BATTLE OF TOURS

In the fall of 732 Charles Martel was campaigning in Germany when he received an urgent message that the Muslims had invaded the Frankish region of Aquitaine in France. He immediately rushed his army west to stop the Muslim advance.

As Martel approached, the Muslims tried to escape home. But they were slowed down by the huge quantities of plunder they had captured. The Franks easily caught up with them near the city of Tours. The Muslim leader, Abd al-Rahman, made ready to attack. Meantime, Martel formed his army into a human wall several men deep.

As the Franks waited, Abd al-Rahman ordered a cavalry charge. Muslim horsemen raced across the battlefield, only to be hurled back by the defenders. Hour after hour the charges continued. The Muslim cavalry could find no way through the Franks.

Then Abd al-Rahman was killed. With their leader dead, the Muslims fell back. They even left their plunder behind. Martel had ended the Muslim threat to Western Europe.

Charlemagne continued to expand the kingdom. He began a long-running series of campaigns against the Saxons in what is now northern Germany. The mostly nomadic, pagan Saxons were old enemies of the Franks. They were always threatening the Franks' borders. Charlemagne was determined to conquer them and in 772 he launched a raid against Saxony. He destroyed a Saxon temple and subdued part of the region. However, the Saxon threat was far from over. Charlemagne's campaign had been successful but the Saxons were to rise up again.

Charlemagne (mounted, at right) accepts the surrender of the Saxon leader Widukind in 785. Charlemagne launched 18 campaigns against the Saxons between 772 and 779.

Full-scale invasion

No sooner had Charlemagne's army left than the Saxons rebelled. Charlemagne responded by launching a full-scale invasion. He was determined to conquer the area and convert the pagan Saxons to Christianity. To keep the Saxons under control, Charlemagne built fortresses. But when the main Frankish army withdrew, the Saxons attacked again.

Charlemagne put down this uprising and another in 778. Then in 782 a rebel Saxon chieftain called Widukind, who had organized the 778 revolt, ambushed and destroyed a Frankish force in the mountains of Saxony. Widukind and his rebels then stormed through Saxony. They destroyed Christian churches and put many Christian priests to the sword.

A furious Charlemagne beheaded 4,500 captured rebels in reprisal. He then crossed into Saxony with his army. His soldiers terrorized the locals and destroyed property at will. His troops stayed on campaign in the depths of winter, even though soldiers usually went home for a rest and to escape the worst of the weather. In 785 Widukind surrendered and the Saxon rebellion ended.

The empire created by Charlemagne covered much of Western Europe and brought a measure of peace and stability to the region unknown since the Roman Empire.

Expanding the empire

The Saxons were not done yet, though, and they revolted again in 793. Once again Charlemagne responded by launching destructive raids into Saxony. But he also moved thousands of Saxons away from their homes and settled them elsewhere. In doing this, he denied the Saxons the manpower they needed to fill the ranks of their armies. Saxon resistance broke under the hammer blows delivered by Charlemagne. Saxony was firmly under Frankish control by 804.

Despite being at war with the Saxons for most of his reign, Charlemagne also managed to expand the Frankish Empire in other directions. In 772 the pope appealed to Charlemagne for help against the Lombard peoples of northern Italy. They were threatening his territories around Rome and elsewhere in Italy. Charlemagne's father had once made a promise of military support to the pope in time of crisis. Charlemagne now honored his father's pledge by marching his forces over the Alps in 773.

He besieged the city of Pavia, the Lombard capital. The Franks had not brought siege weapons with them, however. They had no choice but to starve the city into surrender. The blockade dragged on for many months. It finally ended in June 774. The Lombard king, Desiderius, gave up his kingdom to the victorious Franks. Charlemagne took over his throne.

CHARLEMAGNE AND FEUDALISM

Charlemagne needed huge armies to fight his campaigns. He raised them with the help of his nobles. Each noble was responsible for providing a certain number of men when the king demanded military service. They were to be armed and equipped according to Charlemagne's commands. They were also to bring enough food to keep them supplied on campaign for up to three months.

To begin with, the nobles could call on any free man to fight for the king. But as Frankish armies turned into mainly cavalry forces, the situation began to change. Cavalry equipment and warhorses were expensive. Generally only the richest people or their servants now went on campaign. Foot soldiers were usually only used to garrison towns. They were only sent to war in times of great emergency.

When the Vikings began to raid the empire after Charlemagne's death in 814, the nobles used these cavalry units to defend their lands. The units gradually turned into small semipermanent armies of knights and their personal followers. Weaker neighbors swore loyalty and paid taxes to these nobles in return for their protection. This system of the strong protecting the weak in return for loyalty, as well as money, was called feudalism and lasted in Europe for centuries.

Four years after his defeat of the Lombards Charlemagne launched a long-running campaign against Spain, which was still ruled by Muslims. Muslims were seen as the enemies of Christianity. Muslims from Spain had invaded Frankish territory in the past. Although allied with Muslim rebels, Charlemagne's first expedition failed to make any conquests.

Fighting the Muslims

To make matters worse, Charlemagne's nephew Roland was killed in 778. The Frankish army's supply wagons and its escort commanded by Roland were ambushed at the Pass of Roncesvalles as they made their way back over the Pyrenees Mountains toward the Frankish kingdom. Charlemagne had gone on ahead with the bulk of his army and did not reach his nephew until the battle with the ambushers had ended.

The guard of the Franks' supply wagons had been overwhelmed by the Muslim-led force but Roland had died bravely, facing the enemy with his sword in hand. His heroic death against a stronger foe became the stuff of legend, an epic of courage, and was used in a later medieval poem, *The Song of Roland*.

Conflict with the Muslims continued throughout the rest of the century. The Franks captured a number of towns south of the Pyrenees, the border with Spain. In 795 Charlemagne decided to turn the area in which these towns lay into a buffer zone, or "march," between his kingdom and the Muslims. Castles were built and towns fortified. Charlemagne was also able to capture the port of Barcelona from the Muslims in 801. By 812, when the Muslims asked for peace, the Franks' buffer zone extended from the Pyrenees to the Ebro River in Spain itself.

Charlemagne, the king of the Franks, was a ruler of great ability and was able to expand the Frankish kingdom. His achievements were recognized by Pope Leo III, who crowned him Holy Roman Emperor in 800.

The greatest king of the age

Besides his successes against the Saxons, the Lombards, and the Muslims of Spain Charlemagne also conquered the Avars on the eastern borders of the Frankish kingdom and the Slavs in what is now the Balkans. He also extended the Frankish kingdom deeper into southern Germany. He even crossed swords with the Byzantine Empire far to the east.

Charlemagne was a truly remarkable figure, probably the greatest ruler of the age. Before his reign Western Europe consisted of numerous petty kingdoms that were frequently at war. His successful campaigns brought a measure of peace and security to the region that had not existed since the time of the Romans. Charlemagne used this stability to undertake political and economic reforms, and the arts flourished with his support. However, his successors were far less able than he, and most of his triumphs and achievements were soon lost.

Military reforms

Strangely, despite their conquests, the Franks under Charlemagne fought few pitched battles. The secrets of Carolingian success were siege warfare, the devastation of enemy lands, and the setting up of garrisons to keep conquered people under control. Charlemagne also tried to introduce a range of military reforms. These included defining the military obligations of his nobles, the organization of units, and the weapons and equipment to be carried by individual soldiers. As with his other reforms these farsighted developments were gradually abandoned after his death.

THE VIKING MENACE

At the end of the 8th century bands of violent, warlike seafarers began to terrorize settlements on the coasts of Western Europe. They came from Scandinavia in the far north of Europe. Coming ashore from their longships, these raiders seized any treasure and money they could lay their hands on. They also carried off people to be sold as slaves or to be held for ransom. The Anglo-Saxon people of England had a name for these ferocious raiders. They called them Vikings, meaning pirates.

A sight to strike fear into many Europeans in the early Middle Ages–Viking longships carrying raiders in search of valuable goods and prisoners.

The terror began in the 790s. Gangs of Vikings, who were pagans, attacked coastal monasteries in England, Scotland, and Ireland, and on the mainland of Europe. They were looking for valuables. The raids continued into the 9th century and became more frequent. Vikings from Norway struck mainly at Ireland and Scotland. The Danish Vikings struck at England and what is now France, Belgium, the Netherlands, and Germany. Swedish Vikings raided into what is now Russia and the Ukraine. They reached as far as the Byzantine Empire and Italy.

Raids deep inland

Besides attacking coastal targets, the Vikings also raided inland on foot or on horseback. They even took their longships up rivers or rolled them over land on logs. In 834 they attacked the important port of Dorstadt, 50 miles (80 km) from the sea along the Rhine River in what is now the Netherlands. They returned for more plunder in each of the three following years. In 845 the Vikings traveled up the Seine River as far as Paris. They were given huge amounts of silver to leave the city in peace. Six years later the Vikings sailed up the Elbe River and plundered the rich city of Hamburg in what is now Germany.

To save themselves from having to return home for the winter, the Vikings set up bases near the areas they raided. These bases were often islands in the mouths of large rivers, such as the Loire River in what is now France. When the opposition became too strong in one area or the local ruler paid them to go away, the Vikings would move to another place. In some cases European nobles hired groups of Viking warriors to help them fight off other marauding Viking bands. These "friendly" Vikings were given land and money by the nobles in return for the protection they offered against these other invaders.

VIKING ARMIES

Viking raiders usually carried spears, swords, and axes. They crossed the seas from Scandinavia in longships powered by sail or oars. Early raiders traveled and fought on foot once they had landed. However, faced with cavalry the Vikings had to adopt new tactics. They needed to match the knights for speed. They began to ride to their raiding targets on horseback, although they usually dismounted to fight.

No one really knows how big Viking armies were. The early Viking raids were probably made by small forces, perhaps a single ship carrying 60 men. As time went on, though, raiding forces banded together. By the 850s hundreds of Vikings may have been taking part in raids along the coastline of Europe.

The Great Army (see page 24) that marauded through England and Western Europe was certainly large. However, it is likely that it consisted of only a few thousand men. It certainly never reached the staggering 40,000 Vikings reported by an eyewitness to the siege of Paris in 885.

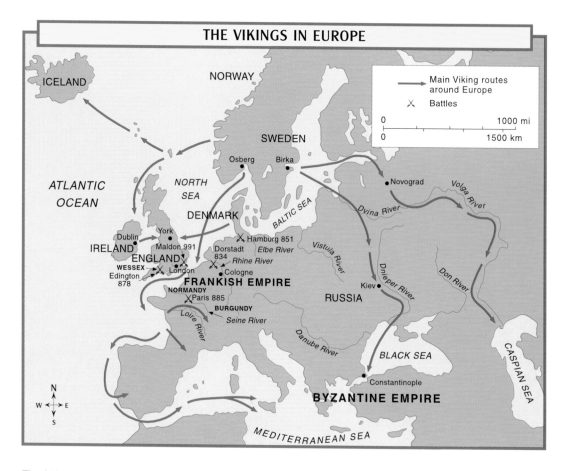

THE VIKINGS IN EUROPE

Main Viking routes around Europe

✗ Battles

0   1000 mi
0   1500 km

ICELAND

NORWAY

SWEDEN

Osberg   Birka

ATLANTIC OCEAN

NORTH SEA

Novograd

Volga River

Dvina River

DENMARK

BALTIC SEA

Dublin   York

IRELAND   Maldon 991

ENGLAND

WESSEX

Edington 878

Hamburg 851

Dorstadt   Elbe River
834   Rhine River

London   Cologne

FRANKISH EMPIRE

NORMANDY

Paris 885

BURGUNDY

Loire River

Seine River

Vistula River

Dnieper River

Kiev

Don River

RUSSIA

Danube River

BLACK SEA

Constantinople

BYZANTINE EMPIRE

CASPIAN SEA

N
W ← → E
S

MEDITERRANEAN SEA

The Vikings were great seafarers and took their longships along many of Europe's major rivers in search of plunder.

In 865 raiding activity quieted down in Ireland and mainland Europe. The Vikings concentrated on England. That year a huge Danish Viking force called the Great Army attacked eastern England. The Vikings captured one fortified English town after another. They used them as bases from which to plunder the surrounding areas. By about 870 the Danes controlled much of the north and east of the country. They then tried to capture the southern English kingdom of Wessex, but here they came up against King Alfred the Great. The war raged until 878, when Alfred finally defeated the Vikings at the Battle of Edington.

After Edington part of the Great Army sailed to mainland Europe. There it began raiding up and down the major rivers once again. In 885 a large Viking army, probably numbering in the thousands, sailed up the Seine, reaching Paris. This time the Vikings attacked the city. Paris was strongly defended, however, and they could not break in.

The siege of Paris lasted 11 months. The Vikings used a giant rock-throwing catapult to try to smash holes in the city walls. They also raided the surrounding area. In the end the Frankish emperor, Charles the Fat, paid the Vikings to leave. They moved farther upriver and rampaged through the region of Burgundy.

Defeat of the Great Army

The Great Army returned to England in 892. The Vikings attacked Wessex once more but Alfred was ready. He had a navy to challenge the Vikings at sea. He had also strengthened the defenses of his towns.

Four years later the Great Army broke up. One group went back to raiding in what is now northern France. In 911 the new Frankish emperor, Charles the Simple, gave land to their leader, Rollo, in return for his loyalty. The area that Rollo and his followers settled was called Normandy. The Vikings and locals intermarried and their descendants became known as Normans.

The remainder of the Viking Great Army moved into northern and eastern England, which was still under Danish rule. Viking bands continued attacking Wessex from there. Early in the 10th century Edward, Alfred's son and the new king of Wessex, began a campaign to reconquer the Danish-controlled areas.

Edward attacked in 909. Every time he captured an area, he built a fortress. The fortresses enabled Edward to control the areas he had conquered and prevented them from falling back into Viking hands. By 954 the Anglo-Saxons had taken back all of the Danish-controlled areas of England.

The return of the Vikings

The Vikings were far from finished. In the 980s the raids on England began again. A large Viking force of 93 ships and perhaps 7,000 men landed in the east of the country and defeated an Anglo-Saxon army at the Battle of Maldon in 991. In 994 this force tried to take London. The Anglo-Saxons paid the Vikings to leave them in peace. However, the Vikings kept coming back. In 1013 King Swein of Denmark launched a full-scale invasion and temporarily added England to his kingdom.

A selection of the weapons and armor used by Vikings in battle. From left to right: the central metal stud of a wooden shield, a sword, and a helmet.

THE NORMAN CONQUESTS

At the start of the 11th century, about 100 years after they had settled in what is now northern France, the Normans began to emerge as a military power in Europe. By now these Viking descendants were Christians and spoke French but they were still warriors at heart. The Normans' first victories were in Italy, although their greatest triumph was the conquest of England in 1066.

From about 1016 onward Norman nobles began traveling to Italy in search of adventure. To begin with they fought as mercenaries in other people's armies. Gradually, though, the Normans took over areas of southern Italy. The increasing power of the Normans in Italy led to war between them and Pope Leo IX, whose territory lay to the north. In 1053 the pope's forces met the Normans at Civitella in southern Italy.

The outnumbered, all-cavalry Norman army lined up in three large bodies—one in the center and one each to the left and right. The right-hand formation under Richard of Aversa charged the pope's cavalry and scattered them. Richard then led his own body of knights around the back of the pope's infantry. The remaining

Norman knights and their valuable warhorses are transported by ship, a remarkable feat beyond the abilities of most of their opponents.

two Norman cavalry formations attacked from the front. Trapping the enemy between their three forces, the Normans eventually won the battle, but only after a bitter struggle. They also captured the pope.

Horses transported by ship

From their territories in southern Italy the Normans next struck at the island of Sicily, which was under Muslim Arab rule. In May 1061 Roger de Hauteville attacked and took the Sicilian city of Messina. Because cavalry was important in the Norman method of warfare, Roger risked transporting his knights' horses from Italy to Sicily by boat. By today's standards such an operation might not seem impressive but in the 11th century carrying warhorses into battle by sea was daring and new.

While Roger began the long task of conquering the rest of Sicily, his elder brother Robert Guiscard expelled the Byzantines from southern Italy. When the Normans first arrived in southern Italy, the region was part of the Byzantine Empire. By 1068 only the port city of Bari on the Adriatic Sea remained under Byzantine control. In August of that year Guiscard laid siege to the city, blocking its harbor mouth with ships. Bari held out for almost three years before it fell.

The Varangian Guard

In 1081 Guiscard laid siege to the Byzantine coastal city of Durazzo (Durrës in what is now Albania). This time he ran into trouble when a huge Byzantine army came to the city's rescue. In the battle that followed the crack Byzantine infantry, the Varangian Guard (themselves of Viking origin), at first drove the Norman cavalry back into the sea. With his army staring defeat in the face, Guiscard rallied his wavering knights for one last effort. He made them try one last, great, battle-winning charge. This scattered the Byzantine forces.

The victory did not belong to the cavalry alone, however. One of the main reasons the Normans were successful in battle was that their cavalry and bowmen had learned to cooperate. When knights and bowmen tried to overcome the enemy independently they struggled. When they worked together, they were awesome. At Durazzo the Norman bowmen played a vital role by

Robert Guiscard tried to carve out a Norman kingdom in southern Italy but died in 1085, leaving the job to be finished by his brother.

pinning down the Varangian axmen, disorganizing their close-packed ranks with their arrows, and giving the knights a chance to prepare for their final charge.

The Byzantines won back Durazzo in 1083, and two years later Robert Guiscard died from disease. In Sicily his brother Roger was going from strength to strength. By 1093 he had conquered the island, leaving it and southern Italy in Norman hands.

Claiming the throne

In January 1066 Edward the Confessor, king of England, died and was succeeded by Harold Godwineson, an Anglo-Saxon noble by birth. However, Duke William of Normandy also claimed to be the rightful king of England because Edward had earlier selected him. In fact, Harold himself had been forced to support William's claim to the English throne after he had been shipwrecked on the Normandy coast and made William's prisoner in 1064. Once back in England, however, Harold had no intention of making way for William. William prepared a large army to invade England and take the crown away from Harold by force.

The conquest of England

Harold knew that William was planning an attack. He stationed troops along the English south coast to keep a close lookout for enemy ships. However, by early September 1066 no sighting of the Norman invasion fleet had been made, and Harold sent his troops home. On the other side of the English Channel, however, the Norman fleet was almost ready to sail. William was waiting for good weather and calm seas before launching his invasion of England.

On September 18 England was attacked—but not from Normandy. Harald Hardrada of Norway, who also wanted to take Harold's place as king, landed in the north of England and

NORMAN KNIGHTS

William of Normandy's main attacking force was his heavy cavalry, made up of armored knights mounted on trained warhorses. Small groups of Norman knights trained together regularly in tournaments. Later they fought side by side on the battlefield.

A Norman knight's armor consisted of a coat of chain mail–closely joined metal rings. He also wore a helmet and carried a long, kite-shaped shield. His weapons were a lance about eight feet (2.6 m) long and a sword, which was flat and used for slashing at the enemy rather than stabbing.

The main heavy cavalry tactic was the massed charge in which the knights rode at the enemy, their lances tucked in under their arms against the body. Another tactic was to pretend to run away. When enemy troops left their defensive line to chase after them, the knights turned around and cut them down with little mercy.

defeated Harold's commanders there at the Battle of Fulford outside the city of York on September 20. Harold, who was in London, rapidly marched his army north. He destroyed Hardrada's forces in a fierce battle at Stamford Bridge just north of York on September 25. No sooner had he done so, though, than Harold had to rush south, via London to pick up troops, to face a new threat. The Normans had landed.

William landed on England's south coast on September 28 and set up a base at Hastings. He sent his troops to raid the local villages to gather food and to provoke Harold into a battle. On October 13 William was told that Harold had arrived in the area from London with his army. It had taken the Anglo-Saxons only

The Battle of Stamford Bridge on September 25, 1066, ended in victory for Harold's Anglo-Saxons. The commander of the invaders, Harald Hardrada, was killed in the fighting.

48 hours to travel the 55 miles (88 km) from London to Hastings —a truly remarkable effort given the poor state of English roads (they were no more than muddy tracks) at the time and the tiredness of his army.

The following day the two forces met at Hastings. The Anglo-Saxons took up position on Senlac Hill, near Hastings, and awaited the Norman onslaught. The battle lasted for several hours and hung in the balance until Harold was wounded and then killed. The Normans then overwhelmed Harold's exhausted men. After the battle the Normans marched on the nearby port of Dover.

Crowned king of England

The Anglo-Saxons refused to surrender London, their capital, to the victorious Normans. To make them change their minds, William once again ordered his troops to raid and terrorize the local people. In the end London opened its gates to the invaders. On Christmas Day 1066 William of Normandy was crowned King William I of England. In the next few years William took control of his new realm. He built castles, from where his nobles ruled the countryside with an iron fist, and he stamped out any rebellion. By 1072 the Norman conquest of England was virtually complete. The Normans set about expanding their new kingdom by invading Wales and settling in various parts of Ireland.

A scene from the Bayeux tapestry, which tells the story of the Norman invasion of England. This section shows mounted Norman knights charging the Anglo-Saxons. This famous tapestry is preserved in a museum in Bayeux, a small town in northwest France.

THE BATTLE OF HASTINGS

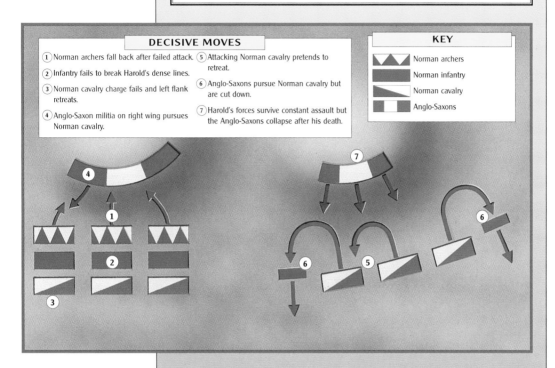

DECISIVE MOVES

1. Norman archers fall back after failed attack.
2. Infantry fails to break Harold's dense lines.
3. Norman cavalry charge fails and left flank retreats.
4. Anglo-Saxon militia on right wing pursues Norman cavalry.
5. Attacking Norman cavalry pretends to retreat.
6. Anglo-Saxons pursue Norman cavalry but are cut down.
7. Harold's forces survive constant assault but the Anglo-Saxons collapse after his death.

KEY

- Norman archers
- Norman infantry
- Norman cavalry
- Anglo-Saxons

On October 14, 1066, the army of William of Normandy attacked King Harold's Anglo-Saxon forces near Hastings. Harold held the high ground. At first the battle did not go well for the Normans. William's bowmen, infantry, and cavalry attacked in turn. But they could do little damage. Harold's foot soldiers, a mixture of trained warriors and local militias, were protected by their shields and armed with spears, swords, and battleaxes.

William ordered sections of his cavalry to pretend to run away in the hope that some defenders would give chase down the hill. When they did, the knights turned and wiped them out. In the meantime Norman bowmen peppered Harold's troops. Some Normans were armed with crossbows, the first time this weapon had been seen in battle in Europe.

As evening approached, an arrow struck Harold in the face. Norman knights finished the king off, leaving the exhausted Anglo-Saxons without a leader. Resistance crumbled, and the remainder of Harold's army fled.

THE CRUSADES: WARS OF RELIGION

In 1071 the Seljuk Turks, the Muslim rulers of the Middle East and Central Asia, defeated the Christian Byzantine emperor at Manzikert. They then swept west, almost to Constantinople. The Seljuks also captured Jerusalem, a place of pilgrimage for Christians. Byzantine emperors appealed to Western Europe for help. In 1095 Pope Urban II responded. Instead of sending the mercenaries the emperor had asked for, the pope called on European Christian soldiers to fight in the Middle East. The Crusades began the next year.

Crusaders attack the walls of Antioch. The city fell on October 3, 1098, after the Crusaders gained entry to a tower thanks to the treachery of one of the Muslim garrison.

During 1096 a number of large Crusader armies from Western Europe began to head east for Constantinople. European nobles, including Bohemond, the son of the Norman leader Robert Guiscard, commanded these armies. He crossed into Seljuk territory in the spring of 1097. The Crusaders' first operation was against the city of Nicaea (Iznik in modern Turkey). Assisted by the Byzantine army, the Crusaders captured the city. They then marched south toward Syria.

The Crusaders panic

On July 1 a Seljuk cavalry force attacked the Crusaders near Doryleum (Eskisehir in modern Turkey). However, instead of carrying lances like European knights, Seljuks were armed with bows. They could fire while riding at speed. They caused panic among the Crusaders, who numbered perhaps 100,000, including civilian pilgrims.

To prevent his forces from being massacred, Bohemond formed a defensive camp. A section of Crusader cavalry attacked the Seljuks from behind as the main force of Crusader knights charged from the front. The result was a Crusader victory. They lost about 4,000 men compared with Seljuk losses of about 3,000.

THE CROSSBOW

The crossbow was one of the most important Crusader infantry weapons. It consisted of a short bow mounted crossways on a length of wood. It was extremely powerful. A Crusader's crossbow could send a bolt (arrow) right through the armor of the time. In fact the crossbow was such a vicious weapon that in 1139 churchmen in Rome declared that it must not be used against Christians. They permitted its continued use against Muslims.

Loading a crossbow took some time, and the bowman needed the aid of a hook carried on his belt. Pointing the weapon toward the ground and anchoring it with his foot, the bowman crouched and slipped the hook over the bowstring. He then slowly stood up, hauling the string with him as he rose until he could hook it over a catch known as a "nut." To operate the weapon the bowman pressed the trigger, releasing the string and sending the bolt toward its target.

The siege of Antioch

Almost four months after the Battle of Doryleum the Crusaders' long march finally brought them to the gates of the city of Antioch, which was in Seljuk hands. Antioch was important to the Crusaders. It was where the first Christian community in the world was established. The city was also strategically important. Traffic moving from Asia Minor to Syria had to pass through it.

The Crusaders besieged Antioch for seven months with little success until Bohemond's spies persuaded a Seljuk officer to let Crusader soldiers in through one of the towers. On June 3, 1098, the Crusaders poured into the city. The fall of Antioch showed

In July 1099, Godfrey de Bouillon (in the red cloak), one of the leaders of the First Crusade, looks out at the city of Jerusalem as news arrives that his troops have stormed the holy city's walls.

the brutal side of the Crusaders. Once inside the city they massacred the Muslim inhabitants and, in their lust for blood, also killed many Christians.

No sooner had the Crusaders moved into Antioch than a Seljuk army arrived outside the city and began to besiege them in turn. After the long Crusader siege there was no food left in Antioch. The Crusaders were soon starving and weak. On June 28, inspired by the discovery of a holy relic in Antioch's cathedral, the Crusaders marched out of the city. The astonished Muslims attacked but were pushed back. The Crusaders then counterattacked and gained the upper hand. Their few thousand men succeeded in driving off the huge Muslim force. The Crusaders were now in control of Antioch.

The capture of Jerusalem

In January 1099 the Crusaders pushed on to Jerusalem. They followed the coast most of the way so that an Italian and English fleet could keep them supplied. By June 7 the Crusaders had arrived outside Jerusalem. The Crusader force was far too small to surround the city and starve it into surrender. The Egyptians, who had captured the city a year before, had also made sure that it was well stocked with supplies. The Crusader leaders— Raymond of Toulouse and Godfrey of Bouillon—decided to take the city by force. They built huge wooden platforms called siege

The Christian states in the Middle East and the major battles and sieges of the Crusades.

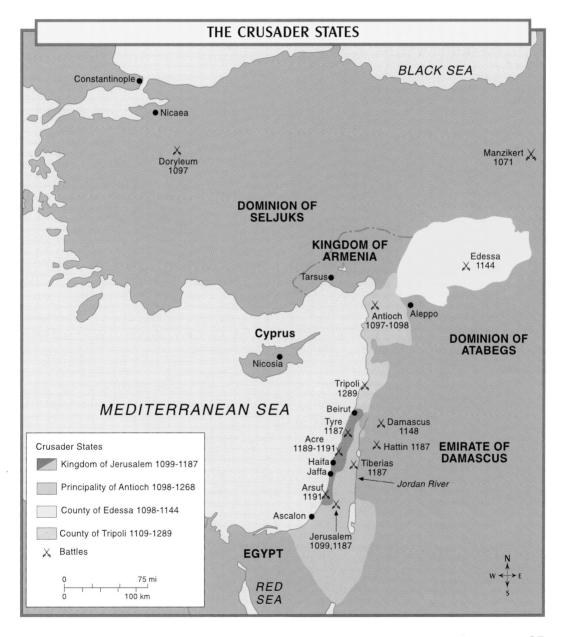

THE CRUSADER STATES

BLACK SEA

Constantinople

Nicaea

Manzikert 1071

Doryleum 1097

DOMINION OF SELJUKS

KINGDOM OF ARMENIA

Edessa 1144

Tarsus

Antioch 1097-1098

Aleppo

Cyprus

DOMINION OF ATABEGS

Nicosia

Tripoli 1289

MEDITERRANEAN SEA

Beirut

Tyre 1187

Damascus 1148

Acre 1189-1191

Hattin 1187

EMIRATE OF DAMASCUS

Haifa
Jaffa

Tiberias 1187

Arsuf 1191

Jordan River

Ascalon

Jerusalem 1099, 1187

EGYPT

RED SEA

Crusader States
- Kingdom of Jerusalem 1099-1187
- Principality of Antioch 1098-1268
- County of Edessa 1098-1144
- County of Tripoli 1109-1289
- ✕ Battles

0 — 75 mi
0 — 100 km

N
W — E
S

towers outside the northern and southern walls. On July 14 the Crusaders pushed their towers up against the walls as the defenders rained down rocks, arrows, and Greek fire. Greek fire is believed to have been a mixture of sulfur, naptha, and quicklime that exploded and burst into flames when wet.

The troops on top of the towers were able to lower drawbridges onto the walls and fight their way into the city. Once inside, the Crusaders went on the rampage as they had at Antioch. They slaughtered the city's Muslim and Jewish inhabitants.

The Crusader states

The following month the Crusaders destroyed a large Egyptian army outside the city of Ascalon. With the help of European fleets, the Crusaders then besieged and captured the major coastal cities of the region, among them Beirut, Haifa, Tripoli, and Tyre. By 1124 the Crusaders controlled all of them except Ascalon, which was held by the Egyptians.

The Crusaders divided their conquests in the Middle East into four states, which consisted of major cities and their surrounding areas. The states were Jerusalem,

Templars were members of one of the religious military orders raised by the Christian kingdoms of Western Europe to protect the Holy Land from the Muslims. Here, they attend a church service.

Antioch, Tripoli, and Edessa, which lay to the northeast of the main Crusader strongholds. Jerusalem controlled the other three states—in theory. In reality Antioch, Tripoli, and Edessa were independent. Bordering the Crusader states were Muslim Seljuk territories. To defend their states, the Crusader rulers had the Military Orders, such as the Templars and the Hospitalers. These were monks who were also knights. The Military Orders manned castles in the Crusader states and supplied cavalry.

In 1127 a new Seljuk governor, Zengi, arrived in the region. In 1144 he recaptured the city of Edessa from the Crusaders. When this news reached Europe, religious leaders called for a campaign to retake the city. King Louis VII of France and Emperor Conrad III of Germany led this new Crusader force,

Armored knights, backed by both archers and crossbowmen, storm the walls of a Middle Eastern town during the Crusades.

which arrived in the Middle East in 1148. Somehow Louis and Conrad persuaded King Baldwin III of Jerusalem to attack the city of Damascus, which was actually an ally of the Crusaders. The pointless operation was a disaster for the Christians and ended the Second Crusade almost as soon as it had begun.

The Seljuks, now commanded by Zengi's son, Nur el-Din, continued to attack the Crusader states. Then, in 1163, the Egyptian chief minister, Shawar, appealed to Nur el-Din for help against his political rivals. Nur el-Din sent an army commanded by his top general, Shirkuh. Shirkuh succeeded in reinstating Shawar but then decided to stay.

Shawar sent for the Crusaders, asking for their help, and a three-year campaign began to keep Shirkuh from taking over Egypt. In 1167 the Crusaders expelled the Seljuks but then tried to conquer Egypt. The Seljuks returned at the Egyptians' request

The Crusaders captured Jerusalem but were unable to hold onto their great prize. Here, Muslim forces led by Saladin take advantage of the Crusaders' weakness and recapture the holy city in October 1187.

and forced the Crusaders to leave. Shirkuh became chief minister but soon died. He was replaced by his nephew, Saladin, who was to prove an outstanding general.

Saladin and holy war

By 1171 Saladin was in complete control in Egypt. When Nur el-Din died in 1174 Saladin took over his empire, sweeping aside all who challenged him. By 1187 Saladin held the major Syrian cities and Egypt. He had the Crusader states surrounded. He then declared a holy war against the Christians.

On July 1 Saladin's huge army crossed the Jordan River and laid siege to the city of Tiberias in the kingdom of Jerusalem. King Guy of Jerusalem responded by sending all the forces at his disposal to raise the siege. On July 4 Saladin crushed the Crusader army at Hattin, leaving Jerusalem and the other states without troops to defend them. Many of the coastal cities soon fell. At the beginning of October Saladin captured Jerusalem. One after the other, castles and strongholds fell as the Crusader states were overrun. Tyre, though, held out against Saladin, aided by reinforcements recently arrived from Europe by sea. In the summer of 1189 the Crusaders struck back against the Muslim, laying siege to the great port of Acre.

The Third Crusade

The loss of Jerusalem to the Muslims resulted in the Third Crusade from Europe. It was led by King Richard I (the Lionheart) of England and King Philip II of France. Philip's forces arrived near Acre in the spring of 1191. Richard landed in June, having conquered the island of Cyprus on the way as a base for Crusader operations in the Middle East.

The Crusaders were still besieging Acre at this point, and Richard immediately took command. He fought off the army that Saladin had sent to the aid of Acre and used the Crusader fleet to cut off supply lines to the city from the sea. A little more than a month later, on July 12, Acre surrendered to the Crusaders.

Richard's prime objective was to retake Jerusalem. To get there Richard led his forces on a long march down the Mediterranean coast. A Crusader fleet accompanied Richard's army. Saladin's troops attacked the Crusaders as they went. They tried to provoke the knights into giving chase so that the Muslims could cut them off from the main force and destroy them when the knights' warhorses tired. Under strict orders from Richard, however, the Crusaders did not respond. Instead they kept on marching. In the end Saladin launched a full-scale assault against the Crusaders.

On the morning of September 7 the Crusaders were marching toward Arsuf,

THE BATTLE OF HATTIN

On July 2, 1187, Saladin, with an army of 30,000, including 12,000 cavalry, captured the city of Tiberias, where Raymond, Crusader count of Tripoli, had his castle. Raymond was not there, but his wife was. Honor demanded that the Crusaders go to her aid.

The following day King Guy of Jerusalem led a Crusader army of about 20,000, including 1,200 knights, on a rescue mission. Saladin's army was waiting and attacked the marching force time and again during the day. That evening, tired and thirsty, the Crusaders camped near a well, only to find that it was dry.

During the night Saladin's troops gave the Crusaders no peace. On the morning of the 4th, as Guy and his army tried to reach the springs at Hattin, the Muslims attacked in force.

In the blistering heat Saladin succeeded in separating the Crusader cavalry from their infantry. Without one another's support the two Crusader arms were helpless. Saladin destroyed them both, winning a great victory.

when a Muslim force of perhaps 20,000 cavalry and infantry struck at the Hospitalers, who were bringing up the rear of Richard's army. The warrior-monks beat the Muslims off as best they could, but Richard refused to allow his forces to attack. Eventually the Hospitalers charged. Richard immediately ordered his knights to charge in support. A wall of cavalry was bearing down on the Muslims. Saladin's troops were pushed back. A further Crusader cavalry charge forced them to withdraw entirely.

Saladin eventually pulled back all the way to Jerusalem. However, although Richard got within sight of the holy city in 1192, he never laid siege to it. The Muslim army was too strong,

SALADIN'S MUSLIM ARMY

The Muslim commander Saladin's army fighting the Crusaders consisted of both professional soldiers and forces drafted in for the campaign. Among the former were the elite units of Saladin's bodyguard. These were cavalry troops. Like Saladin himself they were Kurds from an area that is now occupied by parts of Iran, Iraq, and Turkey, rather than Seljuks or Arabs.

Another mounted group were the Mamelukes, slaves who had been trained as soldiers since childhood. Horse-archers formed a third force. Like the Kurds and the Mamelukes the horse-archers were professionals, but were also mercenaries.

Besides these groups thousands more horsemen were provided by local Muslim rulers who had to give Saladin troops when he needed them. Some of these were also regulars.

Saladin also had infantry, who were chiefly spearmen and archers. The archers used regular bows rather than the crossbows favored by the Crusaders.

Saladin was the greatest Muslim general of the Crusades and equal to any European commander he faced in battle.

KING RICHARD I OF ENGLAND

Richard the Lionheart, king of England between 1189 and 1199, was one of the greatest soldiers of his era. He was an inspiring commander. It was his leadership that enabled the Third Crusade to capture Acre.

Richard was a brave fighter, too. Having heard that Saladin had captured Jaffa in 1192, he personally led a small fleet of boats to the city, jumped into the surf, and waded ashore, fighting as he went. But he could also be ruthless. After the capture of Acre in the summer of 1191, Richard massacred an estimated 3,000 Muslim prisoners, including a large number of women and children.

On his way home from the Crusades Richard was captured by his enemy Leopold V of Austria and held prisoner until England raised the money to pay his ransom. Richard later fought against King Philip II of France, with whom he had gone on crusade. Richard died from an arrow wound at Chalus in France.

and Saladin had destroyed all the crops in the area and poisoned the wells. In September Richard reached an agreement with Saladin. It allowed the Crusaders to remain on the coast of the Middle East and gave Christians the right to visit Jerusalem. Richard then sailed home. Saladin, already ill, died in 1193. The Crusader states survived until 1291, when the Muslims wiped out the last of the Christian settlements on the Mediterranean coast.

King Richard I of England (left) does battle with Saladin. Richard is covered in chain mail, whereas Saladin wears quilted clothing, equally effective protection in combat.

New types of warfare

The Crusades led to improvements in cooperation between cavalry and the infantry in Western Europe. When they arrived in Seljuk territory in 1097, Crusader commanders knew that a cavalry unit was more effective if it worked with infantry. The Crusaders found that they needed to develop this to a higher degree against the Muslims.

Armed with spears and crossbows, the Crusader infantry's task was to defend their knights from attack until they charged. Just before the charge the crossbowmen fired. The Muslims tried to separate the Crusader foot soldiers from the cavalry and deal with each in turn.

MEDIEVAL SIEGE WARFARE

Castles were of very great important in medieval warfare. They were the main headquarters for armies and they were the strongholds from which the nobles controlled their surrounding lands. For these reasons an invading lord or army could not conquer and rule an area without capturing its castle. Because castles were designed to keep even the most determined enemy out, attackers had to develop new, special methods to break in. The struggle between castle defenders and castle attackers is known as siege warfare.

The stone keep (tower) of Cardiff castle in south Wales is a typical example of a Norman design. The keep, which was the most secure area of the castle, was built in the 12th century.

Krak des Chevaliers castle in Syria was captured from the Muslims by the Crusaders in about 1125 and was extensively rebuilt.

Western European nobles started building castles in the 9th century. Some were stone buildings, but more often early castles were wooden towers. In order to give his castle a strong position for defense and for controlling the surrounding countryside, a noble would construct a huge mound (motte) of earth and place the fortress on top of it. To make the castle more difficult to attack, the owner would then dig a ditch around the base of the mound. Larger castles soon began to appear.

The fortress was still a wooden tower on top of a mound, but nobles began to enclose land at the base of the mound by building fences as well as ditches. Between the mound and the fence was a safe area, or bailey, where people lived. These motte and bailey castles were common in Europe.

Motte-and-bailey castles were quick to build—the Normans could construct one in a week. However, a noble needed a large supply of wood to build a timber castle, and his fortress could be

43

CONCENTRIC CASTLES

While they were in the Middle East the Crusaders saw how the Byzantines and Arabs built their castles. The keeps (central stone towers) of their castles were protected by two or three rings of stone walls. Because the rings of walls stood one inside the other, these fortresses became known as concentric castles.

When they came home, the Crusaders built concentric castles in Europe. Usually perched on rocky crags or cliffs, or surrounded by a wide defensive moat, these were among the most complex castles ever built. One of the most outstanding is Harlech castle, constructed in northern Wales during the 1280s by England's King Edward I.

Harlech has an outer wall and then an inner wall with four huge, round towers, one at each corner, enabling defenders to fire down on anyone attacking the inner wall. The castle's strong, well-defended keep-gatehouse was built into this inner wall. The castle was built on top of a high peak to make any attacker's job even more difficult.

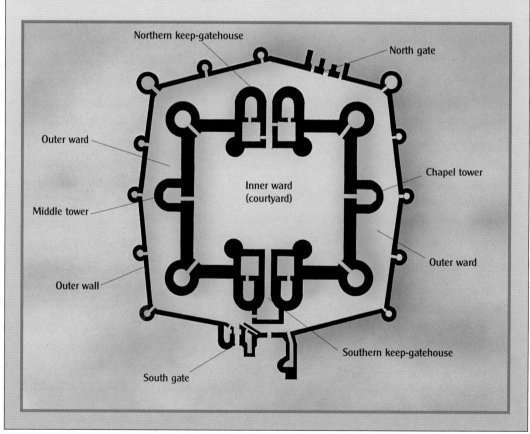

Northern keep-gatehouse

North gate

Outer ward

Chapel tower

Inner ward (courtyard)

Middle tower

Outer ward

Outer wall

Southern keep-gatehouse

South gate

Castles were very difficult to capture. Most fell due to treachery, disease, or hunger rather than assault. However, the introduction of gunpowder artillery signaled the end of the castle. Stone walls could not take the pounding dished out by early artillery. Here, a town is stormed by an army backed by cannon.

destroyed easily by fire. During the 12th century nobles began to build stone castles. Instead of surrounding the bailey with a wooden fence, castle owners now put up stone walls.

Defending the castle entrance

For greater protection nobles filled the ditch around the castle with water to create a moat. They also placed a drawbridge across the moat leading to the castle entrance. When the castle came under attack, the drawbridge could be raised, forcing the enemy to find another way across the moat if they were determined to get in. The entrance to the castle itself was guarded by a well-protected gatehouse, or barbican. The gatehouse was often fitted with a portcullis, a heavy wooden gate that could be lowered to block the doorway. The main fortress of the stone castle was a square tower, or keep. This building was the strongest and best-protected part of all, since the noble and his family and followers locked themselves into this building if the enemy captured the rest of the castle.

First the attackers had to decide how to get into the castle. One choice was to construct siege towers and go over the top of the walls. Siege towers were multistory wooden towers on wheels. Soldiers pushed them up to the walls. Other troops at the top then lowered a type of drawbridge that enabled them to cross onto the tops of the walls and break into the castle.

Attackers could try to bring down a castle's walls. They could use rock-throwing weapons to smash holes in them. They could use a battering ram to punch a way through. Defenders fired at the battering ram, so it was necessary to build a kind of armored shed over the ram to protect both it and its operators.

Mining operations

Another way of destroying castle walls was by mining. Mining was carried out by engineers called sappers. They dug beneath the castle walls and propped up the roofs of their tunnels with wooden supports. They then set fire to them. As they burned, the roofs of the tunnels caved in, bringing down the walls above and making a hole in the castle's defenses. Moats made mining operations more difficult. Defenders sometimes dug into the sappers' tunnels from inside the castle and stopped their work.

Attacking armies had to be on their guard during a siege. The defenders could shoot at them from the wall. They could send out forces to strike at the besiegers and burn their siege weapons. Because of these dangers, attacking armies sometimes built fences or walls in front of themselves as protection against the castle defenders. The attackers had to keep watch for armies coming to the castle's rescue. To protect themselves from a rescuing army, the attackers sometimes built a wall behind themselves as well.

If the attackers succeeded in breaking into a castle, the rules of war of the time allowed them to loot and plunder. Of course, the attackers were not always able to break in. Sometimes the only way to capture a castle was to blockade it. Blockading meant cutting off the castle and making sure no supplies got through to it.

SIEGE WEAPONS

A number of siege weapons existed before the invention of firearms. Among them was the ballista, a huge arrow-firing crossbow. Another was the mangonel, which was a catapult with a vertical throwing arm. Soldiers wound back the mangonel's throwing arm and placed a stone ball in a type of cup at its tip. They then released the arm, which flew forward and launched the missile at the enemy.

The trebuchet was a third kind of siege weapon. Like the mangonel it had a vertical throwing arm but it worked in a slightly different way. One tip of the trebuchet's throwing arm carried a sling that contained the missile; the other tip had a huge weight on the end. When the throwing arm was released, the weight dropped suddenly. The arm flew over, releasing the missile toward its target.

Although siege weapons usually threw stone balls to smash castle walls, they sometime lobbed dead horses and bodies into besieged castles to spread disease among the defenders and lower their morale. They also lobbed burning bundles of cloth or wood to set fire to a castle's wooden buildings or rafters.

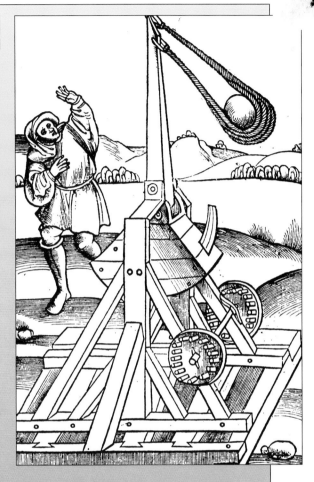

A medieval wooden catapult in action. The missile, here a rock, is placed in a sling (top right) and then flung forward in an arc by releasing a heavy counterweight.

The aim was to starve the garrison into surrender. A determined and well-stocked castle could hold out against even a well-equipped army for a long time, though.

The arrival of effective gunpowder firearms in the 15th century changed siege warfare. Large cannon, such as bombards, could smash through the strongest walls. Castles simply could not stand up to these weapons. Sieges no longer took weeks, months, or years—they could be over in a matter of days.

THE MONGOL INVASIONS

In the early 13th century a great new military menace exploded out of Central Asia. Tough, disciplined, and with a reputation for cruelty, the nomadic Mongols swept all before them. Their enormous forces were almost entirely mounted on sturdy horses. The Mongol armies moved swiftly, living off the land as much as their own supplies. No one, it seemed, could withstand the onslaught of the all-conquering Mongol hordes.

In 1206 Genghis, great khan (leader) of the Mongols, embarked on a campaign of expansion that changed the face of Asia and Eastern Europe. He began by invading China, at that time divided into a number of empires. Genghis struck first at the Western Hsia Empire, taking it under his control in 1209. He then attacked the Chin Empire. He broke through the Great Wall of China and crushed the Chin armies in battle.

Genghis Khan (top, second from left) founded a great Mongol Empire that spread from Central Asia to the borders of Eastern Europe.

Mongol forces consisted of fast-riding horse troops. They usually aimed to surround their enemies and then overwhelm them with volleys of arrows and cavalry charges. This was fine in the field, but the Chin then withdrew into their walled cities. The Mongols needed to develop their siegecraft to capture the cities. They learned fast. Genghis built up his siege equipment, including catapults, battering rams, and scaling towers.

Cities fall to the Mongols

Trouble on the western edge of the Mongol Empire in 1217 forced Genghis to halt his campaign in China temporarily. He went to war with the Khwarizmians. Four Mongol armies rode into Khwarizm, southeast of the Caspian Sea, from the east. Genghis circled Khwarizm and swept in from the west, a surprise move that stunned the Khwarizmians by its speed and brutality. The Mongols quickly captured and then sacked several major Khwarizm cities, including Samarkand.

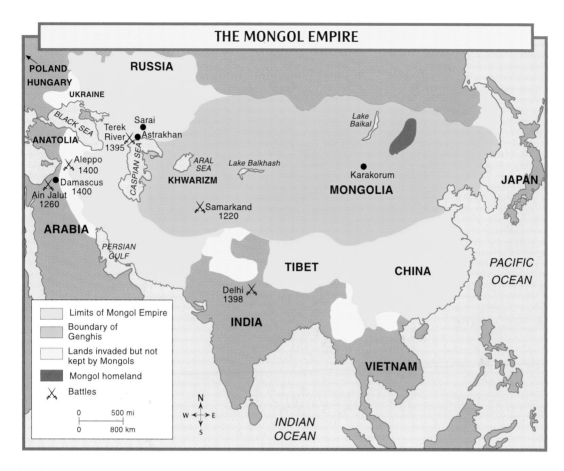

THE MONGOL EMPIRE

By 1224 the Mongols had conquered Khwarizm and were able to turn their attention to China once again. In 1226 they put down an uprising by the Western Hsia and then attacked the Chin again. The following year, though, Genghis died. At a great gathering in Mongolia, his son Ogatai was chosen to succeed him. Ogatai had ambitious plans. He prepared to attack Europe.

The Mongols move west

Ogatai launched his invasion of Europe in 1237. That winter armies commanded by his nephews Batu and Mangu and the great general Subotai poured west into Russia and the Ukraine. Within months the Mongols had taken northern Russia. By early 1241 they had overrun the whole of Russia and the Ukraine.

The Mongols then moved westward into Poland and Hungary. That spring they captured the Polish city of Cracow and burned it to the ground. They then inflicted two defeats on

From their homeland in Central Asia the Mongols swept through China, the Middle East, Russia, and reached Eastern Europe. The empire did not last, however, because of infighting and a lack of strong central leadership.

49

Some 40,000 Germans and Poles fought the Mongols at the Battle of Liegnitz on April 9, 1421. The Europeans put up stubborn resistance but were eventually smashed. The Mongols also lost heavily but continued to devastate much of Eastern Europe.

the Europeans. Ogatai's grandson, Kaidu, defeated an army under Henry of Silesia at Liegnitz in Poland. Subotai smashed a Hungarian force at the Sajo River in northeast Hungary.

The whole of Europe was at the Mongols' mercy. Suddenly, however, Subotai ordered his armies to turn back. Ogatai had died. In keeping with Mongol custom his family, including many generals, returned to Mongolia to choose a successor.

Despite the withdrawal from Europe the Mongol Empire continued to expand under Ogatai's successors. In 1243 the Mongols defeated the Seljuks and took control of Anatolia (part of modern Turkey). During the reign of Mangu they conquered areas of the Middle East and began campaigns against Vietnam.

By now the overall Mongol Empire consisted of four smaller empires. The empire of the Golden Horde included northwestern Asia and Russia. The Jagatai Khanate consisted of much of Central Asia. Persia and southwest Asia were known as the the Il-Khanate. The region around the Mongol capital, Karakorum, was the empire of the great khan, who controlled the other three.

After Mangu's death the Mongol Empire began to fall apart. The three khanates become independent of Karakorum. In 1260 the empire in the west received a setback when a Mongol force was defeated by the Muslims at Ain Jalut. In the east the situation was more encouraging. In 1279 Kublai, Mangu's successor as great khan, won the war in China that Genghis had started. Kublai proclaimed himself emperor of China.

There was one major wave of Mongol expansion at the end of the 14th century It was the work of one of the most ruthless Mongol leaders—Tamerlane. Tamerlane's base was Samarkand in the Jagatai Khanate. In 1369 he overthrew the Jagatain khan and then conquered the Il-Khanate. Tamerlane set his sights on the Golden Horde. Its khan, Toktamish, was his enemy. Tamerlane defeated Toktamish at the Battle of the Terek River in 1395. Tamerlane then destroyed the cities of Astrakhan and Sarai.

The Mongols in decline

Tamerlane's next target was India. He attacked in 1398 and reached Delhi. The city felt the full force of the Mongol terror even though it surrendered. The Mongols stacked the heads of their victims at the city gates. Tamerlane next led his army into Egypt and Anatolia. Tamerlane died in 1405. The Ming dynasty had already overthrown the Mongols in China, the Il-Khanate was gone, and Tamerlane had destroyed the Golden Horde and the Jagatai Khanate. The age of Mongol conquest was over.

THE MONGOL WAR MACHINE

Genghis Khan's huge armies consisted almost wholly of cavalry. The heavy cavalry wore armor and carried lances. Their role was to charge the enemy. The unarmored light cavalry, about 60 percent of the army, carried out reconnaissance and patrol work. They also bombarded the enemy with arrows and javelins before heavy cavalry charges. The Mongols were the best-trained and best-disciplined mounted troops of their time.

Mongol warfare was based on mobility. Each lightly equipped cavalryman went into action with spare horses. Each Mongol warrior changed to a fresh horse whenever he needed.

Their legendary mobility was backed up by excellent intelligence work. For example, the Mongols carried out an expedition against Russia in the 1220s and used the information they gathered to plan their full-scale invasion of 1237.

THE HUNDRED YEARS WAR

In the 1330s the English king, Edward III, held lands in France since he was related to the French royal family. In England Edward was the absolute ruler. In his French territory of Aquitaine, however, he was not. He was a subject of the French king, Philip VI, who owned Edward's lands there. Edward did not like this and was determined to be sole master of Aquitaine. The French king knew of Edward's aims and was determined to stop him. The quarrel between England and France lasted, on and off, for over 100 years.

Naval warfare in the Hundred Years War was virtually identical to the battles fought at sea during ancient times. There was no attempt to maneuver, and soldiers tried to capture enemy vessels in bloody hand-to-hand combat.

The French were particularly unhappy at how much influence England had in the French territory of Flanders. At the same time England was furious at the help France was giving to Scotland in its wars against the English. In 1337 these quarrels led to the first outbreak of hostilities between England and France. Historians today call this prolonged conflict the Hundred Years War.

King Philip of France sparked the conflict. He claimed that the English king was a disobedient and rebellious subject and tried to take away Edward's lands in Gascony, an area of Aquitaine. Gascony was a rich area, since it was a center of the wine trade. It made England plenty of money.

Edward could not afford to lose Gascony and prepared for war. He declared that according to the laws of inheritance, he and not Philip was the rightful king of France. In 1339 Edward began his military campaign. He led a raiding force across the English Channel and devastated the northeast of France. When Philip arrived with the French army, Edward, who had too small a force to give battle, withdrew and sailed home.

Edward planned to return to France, but first he had to do something about the French navy. French ships had raided the southern English coast in 1338 and 1339. In the summer of 1340 Edward heard that Philip was gathering a huge fleet on the coast of Flanders.

Edward seized his chance. He sailed the English fleet across the Channel, took the French by surprise, and smashed their 200-ship force at Sluys. Edward then laid siege to St. Omer and Tournai. Unable to force either of the towns to surrender, however, he made peace with Philip and sailed for England once again.

The peace did not last, though. In 1345 Edward sent a force of 2,500 troops to Gascony, following a French invasion of English territory there. The following year Edward landed in Normandy in northern France with a highly organized army of about 20,000 men.

The Crécy campaign

Edward quickly decided to help his army in Gascony. He hoped his invasion would force the French to send troops from Gascony to oppose him in the north. Edward immediately began a campaign of devastation to provoke the French into attacking him. His men rode through the countryside looting and burning. The French forces stayed in Gascony, but Philip put an army on alert in Paris and prepared to attack the English.

Outnumbered, Edward turned away from Paris and headed for Flanders, which was now an ally of England. With Philip snapping at his heels, Edward found his way north barred by the Seine and Somme Rivers. He crossed them in the nick of time and then, realizing he could not outrun his pursuers, turned to face the approaching French forces.

Throughout August 26 the English army prepared for battle, setting up defensive positions on a ridge near Crécy. Edward split his force into three divisions, each made up of knights and men-at-arms on foot and archers. Edward protected his troops from cavalry attack by placing rows of sharpened wooden stakes in front of them.

THE BATTLE OF SLUYS

In response to French naval raids on the English ports of Portsmouth and Southampton, Edward III led the English fleet across the Channel on June 24, 1340. At about noon on the 24th he attacked the French navy at Sluys. The English had 150 to 180 ships. The French had about 200.

Sluys was not like a modern naval battle, with ships pounding one another from a distance with guns or missiles. Instead the two fleets drew up alongside one another, and soldiers on board the ships fought exactly as they would have done on land. The English archers exchanged shots with the Genoese crossbowmen fighting for the French. Then knights and men-at-arms (the knights' trained retainers) armed with spears, swords, shields, and axes engaged in combat.

Edward and the English won a decisive victory, destroying or capturing almost all the French vessels. Among these was the *Christopher*, which was armed with four cannon. It seems that the *Christopher's* crew did not use these weapons in the battle.

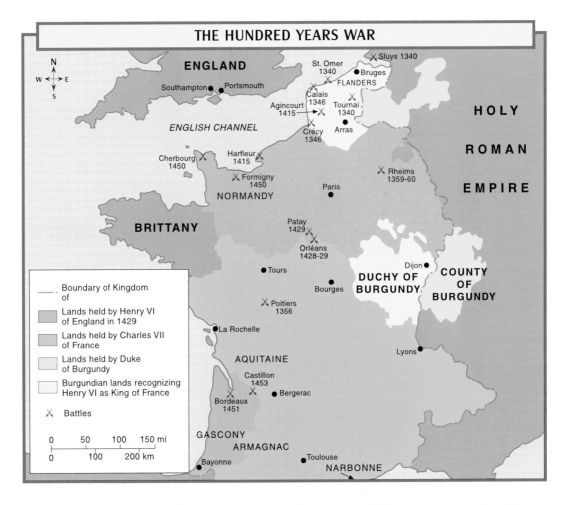

THE HUNDRED YEARS WAR

ENGLAND

Southampton
Portsmouth

St. Omer 1340
Bruges
Sluys 1340
FLANDERS

Calais 1346
Agincourt 1415
Tournai 1340
Arras

ENGLISH CHANNEL

Crécy 1346

HOLY

ROMAN

Cherbourg 1450
Harfleur 1415
Rheims 1359-60

Formigny 1450
Paris

NORMANDY

EMPIRE

BRITTANY

Patay 1429

Orléans 1428-29

Dijon
Tours
DUCHY OF BURGUNDY
COUNTY OF BURGUNDY

Bourges

Poitiers 1356

La Rochelle

Lyons

AQUITAINE

Castillon 1453

Bergerac

Bordeaux 1451

Legend:

— Boundary of Kingdom of

◻ Lands held by Henry VI of England in 1429

◻ Lands held by Charles VII of France

◻ Lands held by Duke of Burgundy

◻ Burgundian lands recognizing Henry VI as King of France

✕ Battles

| 0 | 50 | 100 | 150 mi |
| 0 | 100 | 200 km |

GASCONY

ARMAGNAC

Bayonne
Toulouse
NARBONNE

The Hundred Years War saw the English enjoy the better of the fighting in its earlier years, but the French rallied under Joan of Arc in the late 1420s and they were finally victorious in the 1450s.

The French army of about 60,000 caught up with Edward that evening. Philip sent his crossbowmen ahead to soften up the English line. These skilled soldiers were mercenaries from the Italian city of Genoa. However, they came under such a torrent of English arrows that they retreated. As the crossbowmen turned back, the French cavalry, following up behind, rode over the top of them, trampling many of them underfoot. The French attack turned to chaos.

As arrows continued to rain down, wave after wave of French cavalry rushed headlong at the English defenses. Some French horsemen managed to reach the English lines, only to be stopped by Edward's dismounted knights and men-at-arms who charged out from behind the sharpened stakes and killed the French knights who were easy prey.

THE LONGBOW: THE DECISIVE WEAPON

The Welsh invented the longbow, and Edward I, Edward III's grandfather, introduced it into the English army. The longbow was simple. It was a length of tapering wood about six feet (2 m) long with a single string running from end to end. Even so it was a fearsome weapon and had advantages over the crossbow, which the French army favored.

The longbow had about twice the range of a crossbow, since it could kill a man at 250 yards (230 m). It also had a more rapid rate of fire. A skilled longbowman could fire between six and 12 arrows a minute. To reload all he had to do was pull the bowstring back. Crossbow strings at the time of Crécy were so tight that they had to be wound back with a crank, which took time.

The longbow was at least as powerful as the crossbow and could send an arrow through most armor of the day. Special arrowheads were used to punch through armor or attack horses.

Longbowmen exchange fire with crossbowmen during the Battle of Crécy in 1346. The longbow's greatest advantage over the crossbow was its rate of fire. However, English longbowmen had to spend many hours training to perfect their archery skills.

When the fighting ended at nightfall, thousands of French troops, including 1,500 knights and nobles, lay dead on the battlefield. Crécy signaled the beginning of the end of the armored knight as the dominant medieval soldier. The battle won, Edward marched north and laid siege to the coastal town of Calais. He wanted a port on the French coast opposite England so that he could move troops in and out of France. After a year's blockade by land and sea, Calais surrendered.

The Black Prince campaigns

The terrible disease known as the Black Death plague arrived in Western Europe in the 1340s. England and France stayed at peace until the plague died down. In 1355 the fighting resumed. Edward organized a series of raids in northern and southwestern France. His son, Edward the Black Prince, directed operations in the southwest. Toward the end of the year the prince led a three-month expedition across much of southern France, campaigning from Bordeaux to Narbonne.

Almost unopposed by French forces, his army stormed and burned a number of towns before returning to base with a huge quantity of plunder. The next summer the Black Prince set out on another destructive raid, this time into central France. After several weeks of terrorizing the countryside he reached the city of Tours on the Loire River. There he learned that a French army was closing in on him. He turned back at once, but his baggage train laden with plunder slowed him down. The French caught up with the Black Prince near the town of Poitiers. He had no choice but to fight.

The Black Prince placed his 12,000-man army in a solid defensive position with a vineyard to the front, a small wood to the rear, and swampy ground on the left. His main defensive line consisted of dismounted knights and men-at-arms. Archers lay hidden behind every vine and hedge.

The French attacked on the morning of September 19, beginning with a cavalry charge that was cut down by the Black Prince's bowmen, who shot the horses. The second French cavalry division then advanced on foot. Without their horses these armored troops were clumsy and slow. Even so some reached the English lines and engaged the Black Prince's forces. After a hard hand-to-hand struggle the English drove the French back, but not before both sides had suffered heavy losses. This was a decisive turning point, but the battle was fought to the bitter end.

A royal prisoner

The third French wave, seeing the bloody destruction ahead of them, withdrew from the battlefield. The fourth division, commanded by the king himself, marched into the attack. Instead of waiting for the French to arrive, the Black Prince ordered his troops to charge. At the same time he sent a cavalry force around the outside of the advancing French to strike at them from behind. The French were caught between the frontal assault and the cavalry attack and were defeated. About 3,000 French troops died at Poitiers. Many were taken prisoner, among them King John II, who had succeeded Philip VI in 1350.

Edward III was still determined to be crowned king of France. But when his winter campaign of 1359–1360 failed to take the important French city of Rheims, he finally dropped his claim to the French throne. In the peace talks that followed the French agreed to grant Edward an enormous area of southwest France, not as a subject of the king of France but as its sole overlord. The French also agreed to hand over a huge ransom in return for their captive king, although John II in fact died before he could be released by the English.

The climax of the Battle of Poitiers. King John of France, surrounded by his English enemies, is protected by England's Black Prince. The French king became a valuable prisoner, worth much more alive than dead to the English.

The French commander Bertrand du Guesclin was, unusually, not of noble birth. He avoided battle against the English and waged a successful guerrilla war against their French bases.

An uneasy peace

England and France were now at peace, but the French people continued to suffer. With no war to fight the French army dismissed its mercenary units. These groups now roamed the countryside, terrorizing and robbing the population.

In 1368 the nobles of Gascony rebelled against their English overlords and their heavy taxes. When the French king, Charles V, sided with the rebels, Edward III claimed the throne of France once again, and war erupted. The English invaded northern France. They tried their tactic of looting the countryside in an attempt to provoke the French into a battle. It did not work.

Under the orders of Bertrand du Guesclin, Charles V's top general, the French shut themselves in castles and fortified towns. There was no one for the English troops to terrorize and little plunder. A French army followed the English wherever they went and harassed them. The French wore the English down with frequent ambushes and raids, but avoided taking part in full-scale battles.

The English were also losing their hold on their territories in southwest France. French troops besieged and captured town after town. By the time he died in 1377 Edward III had little more than the lands he had held right at the beginning of the war in 1337. The French were now on top. Although fighting continued on and off almost to the end of the century, the war was fizzling out. In 1396 France and England signed a 30-year truce that they hoped would bring the war to an end.

The peace lasted until 1415, when Henry V, who was now king of England, invaded France. Henry, a dynamic and vigorous monarch, was determined to become the king of France. He struck while the French were fighting a war against the duke of Burgundy, with whom Henry had made an alliance.

THE BATTLE OF AGINCOURT

On October 25, 1415, Henry V advanced slowly toward the huge French force blocking his route to Calais. A short distance from the French Henry stopped and took up a defensive position. He placed dismounted knights and men-at-arms in the center and his archers on the left and right. Sharpened wooden stakes were placed in front of his line to prevent the mounted French knights from getting to close quarters.

The French launched a cavalry charge. As at Crécy and Poitiers the English archers cut the French horsemen to ribbons. Next, a wave of French cavalrymen came forward on foot. The battlefield, a plowed field, was muddy and narrow. The slow-moving French were so tightly packed together they could hardly move their arms. Eventually they clashed with the English defensive line. But as they did so, unarmored archers began swarming around the clumsy, metal-clad knights, striking at them with axes, knives, and swords.

The second dismounted French wave also suffered badly. Scarcely any of the third wave attacked. Henry then scattered the remaining French forces with a cavalry charge. His 6,000-strong army had beaten a French force five times its size. Some 5,000 French were killed, while the English lost little more than 100.

Agincourt was the greatest victory won by foot soldiers against armored knights.

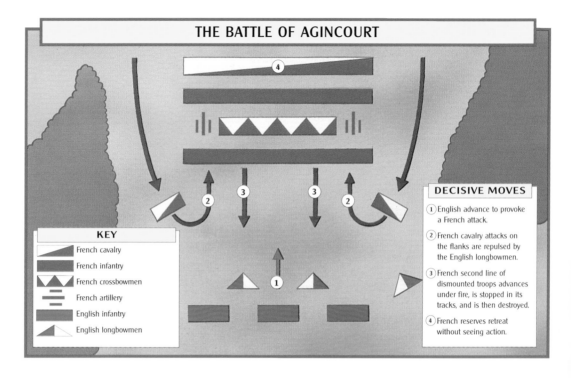

THE BATTLE OF AGINCOURT

KEY

- French cavalry
- French infantry
- French crossbowmen
- French artillery
- English infantry
- English longbowmen

DECISIVE MOVES

1. English advance to provoke a French attack.
2. French cavalry attacks on the flanks are repulsed by the English longbowmen.
3. French second line of dismounted troops advances under fire, is stopped in its tracks, and is then destroyed.
4. French reserves retreat without seeing action.

The Battle of Agincourt in 1415, a great English victory, was also a decisive reminder that the age of the noble, armored knight was coming to an end. Trained soldiers, men considered by the nobility to be little better than possessions, were becoming far superior to the great lords mounted on their warhorses.

Henry landed in Normandy in August. He laid siege to the town of Harfleur, which surrendered the following month. The English army then set off on a 120-mile (192-km) march across northern France to Calais, which was still an English possession. In order to reach Calais Henry had to cross the Somme River. He struggled to find a crossing. Eventually he succeeded in getting across the river, but he then ran into the French king's army near Agincourt. The English force of 6,000 was outnumbered by 30,000 French. Even so Henry won an amazing victory.

Two kings die

Henry halted his campaign after Agincourt. Two years later, once his navy had gained control of the English Channel, he invaded France again. This time he had come to conquer. Within two years he controlled the whole of Normandy. He then set his sights on conquering northern France. In August 1422, however, Henry suddenly got sick and died. He was succeeded by his son, Henry VI.

Just weeks after Henry V's death the French king, Charles VI, also died. The duke of Burgundy and his family, allies of the English, immediately declared Henry VI of England to be the new French king. Burgundy's civil war enemies, meanwhile, supported Charles VI's son, who claimed to be King Charles VII of France. The English were determined to crush Charles VII. By 1428 they had conquered all of northern France and had the upper hand in the rivalry. They planned to invade the south, Charles VII's stronghold. In October 1428 the English attacked the city of Orléans, the border between the English-ruled and French-ruled lands.

Joan of Arc inspires the French

The French withdrew into the fortified city. The English brought siege weapons from Paris and began a blockade. The besiegers had only about 5,000 men. The French, who outnumbered

Joan of Arc, a peasant woman, proved a greater inspiration to the French than any of the country's male leaders. She scored a major victory at Orléans in 1429 but became a victim of the complex politics of the age and was burned at the stake.

EARLY GUNPOWDER WEAPONS

The first time guns were fired in a European battle was when Edward III's English army used three small cannon against the French at the Battle of Crécy in 1346. They do not seem to have played much of a part in Edward's victory.

Armies were more likely to use early gunpowder weapons in siege warfare than in pitched battles. They were usually heavy, difficult to move, inaccurate, and prone to explode.

By the beginning of the 15th century there were many different types of guns. Among them were culverins, which were fairly small cannon, and bombards, big guns used for smashing city walls. At the siege of Constantinople in 1453 the Turks had a cannon that could hurl a large stone ball more than a mile (1.6 km).

Handguns also existed in the 1450s. However, they did not become widely used until the next century. These guns consisted of a metal tube fitted to a wooden handhold. They were fired by applying a lighted match made from cord or rag, which was covered in saltpeter.

They were difficult to load and operate. Even a trained soldier would find it difficult to aim and fire these early handguns with any accuracy at anything beyond very close range. The guns often exploded, killing the user.

them, did not try to break out because they were terrified of English skill on the battlefield. The siege wore on with no end in sight. In April 1429 a French army finally arrived to the rescue.

The French force included Joan of Arc, a peasant girl who believed God had sent her to drive the English from France. Joan inspired the French troops. On May 5 the French attacked and captured one of the three forts the English had built to blockade Orléans. Over the next two days the French defeated the English troops manning the other forts and forced them to withdraw.

The English defeated

Their victory at Orléans gave the French heart. The following month they came across the English army near the village of Patay. On Joan's suggestion, the French launched a cavalry charge. The surprise attack overran the English. Joan, however, was captured by England's Burgundian allies in 1430. The English burned her at the stake the next year. Even so the French now held the advantage. England's hold on France was weakening. When the Anglo-Burgundian alliance ended in 1435, it was only a matter of time before the French drove the English out.

After a five-year truce from 1444 to 1449 the French attacked English-held territory in Normandy. At Formigny in 1450 the French used cannon to defeat an English army armed with longbows. Skill with the longbow had been a major reason for English success at Crécy, Poitiers, and Agincourt. But longbows were no match for cannon and a much better trained French army.

Bordeaux pounded by artillery

The English strongholds in Normandy fell one by one. When Cherbourg surrendered in August 1450, English rule in northern France was finished, although England kept Calais until 1558. Parts of the southwest were still under English control. In June 1451 the French used artillery to capture Bordeaux, and French artillery destroyed an English army at Castillon in July 1453. The Hundred Years War really was over.

The Hundred Years War pointed the way to the future. The French developed gunpowder weapons that proved highly effective. The English, victors in many battles because of the longbow, failed to see the potential of these new weapons and did not fully appreciate their power.

THE RISE OF THE OTTOMANS

In the 14th century a Muslim Turkish people called the Ottomans rose to power in the former Seljuk region of Anatolia. They took control of most of Anatolia by conquering their neighbors and then invaded the Balkans in southeast Europe. By the early 15th century the Ottomans controlled much of the Balkans. Even Constantinople, capital of the once-mighty Byzantine Empire, was in danger of falling into their hands. Then, in 1402, the Mongol warlord Tamerlane crushed the Ottomans at the Battle of Ankara in Anatolia.

Tamerlane's victory in Anatolia allowed many local rulers there and in the Balkans to regain their independence from the Ottomans. From 1413 Sultan Mehmed I brought most of Anatolia and the Balkans back under Ottoman control, however. When he died in 1421, his son, Sultan Murad II, continued his father's work.

Five-year naval war

Murad's first campaign was against the Venetians. The Venetians, from the Italian city of Venice, were powerful in the Mediterranean area at the time. In 1423 the tottering Byzantine Empire granted Venice control of the city of Thessalonika in what is now Greece. This worried Murad. He thought that Venice was becoming too powerful and was challenging Ottoman power. So, in 1425 he launched his armies against the Venetians in Thessalonika.

Sultan Mehmed II (shown here), called "the Conqueror," was an able and energetic king. He expanded the empire rebuilt by his grandfather, Mehmed I, and his father, Murad II. His great triumph was the capture of the city of Constantinople in 1453 (see page 68).

THE EARLY OTTOMAN EMPIRE

Murad's action sparked a five-year naval war between the Ottomans and the Venetians. In the end though, Murad took Thessalonika and slaughtered many of the city's defenders.

Murad then turned his attention to Hungary. For years the Hungarians had been trying to weaken Ottoman control in the Balkans. In 1441 Murad crossed the Danube River and invaded Hungary. This campaign turned out to be a mistake, for Murad came up against a gifted Hungarian general, John Hunyadi. Hunyadi pushed the Ottomans back over the Danube.

The extent of the Ottoman Empire in the latter part of the 15th century. The greatest Ottoman victory of the period came in 1453 when the forces of Mehmed II captured the great city of Constantinople.

The final crusade

The pope and the Byzantines were worried about having a Muslim Ottoman Empire in southeast Europe. Therefore, in January 1443 Pope Eugenius IV announced a Crusade against the Ottomans. He called on Christians to go to war to save the Balkans and Constantinople from the Ottoman threat. John Hunyadi led his Crusader army over the Danube and into Ottoman territory. That summer the Crusaders captured several Ottoman cities. At the same time Murad's enemies attacked his territories in the east. Facing a war on two fronts, the sultan had to make peace with the Hungarians and his eastern enemies.

The Hungarians withdrew—but not for long. In August 1444 Hunyadi marched into Ottoman territory with 20,000 men. The Europeans knew Murad's army was in Anatolia. A Venetian fleet

65

Janissaries were the elite infantry of the Ottoman Empire. They had particularly fancy uniforms, although the headdresses seen here were worn only on ceremonial occasions.

was sent to stop the Ottomans from crossing into Europe as well as also link up with Hunyadi's forces at Varna on the Black Sea coast. The Venetian fleet did not succeed. The Ottomans were left free to march into Europe.

On November 10 a huge Ottoman army arrived at the city of Varna. The Crusaders were waiting for them. But this time it was Hunyadi's turn to make a mistake. He ordered the Crusaders to attack the Ottomans head-on. His men were thrown back in chaos. Murad's forces then went on the offensive. They quickly defeated the Crusaders. Hunyadi was one of the few Europeans who escaped, but their was no disguising the severity of the defeat inflicted on the Christians by the Ottomans.

The Crusade against the Ottomans was over. But Hunyadi was not finished yet. In 1448 Hunyadi once again invaded Ottoman territory, this time with a Hungarian army of about 25,000. Murad replied immediately by marching 100,000 men to meet the Hungarians and push Hunyadi back.

The two armies met at Kossovo on October 16. Murad placed his heavy cavalry units on the left and right sides of his battle line. In the center he deployed his crack infantry, the Janissaries. Janissaries were slave-soldiers. They were born Christians but were made slaves as boys and then brought up as Muslims. The Janissaries were excellent, loyal soldiers and were much feared by the Ottomans' enemies. In the early days of the Ottoman Empire the elite corps of Janissaries numbered about 10,000 men but in later centuries their numbers would be expanded greatly.

Bows against firearms

In the meantime Hunyadi formed his outnumbered army in a similar way opposite the Ottomans. He placed his cavalry to the left and right and his infantry in the center. But Hunyadi's infantrymen were excellent German mercenaries. They carried firearms instead of the bows used by the Ottomans.

The Battle of Kossovo lasted for two days. In the center the Janissaries and the German mercenaries slugged it out with their bows and handguns. Both were protected by a wooden palisade (fence of strong stakes) and they exchanged fire at a range of no more than 100 yards (93 m). But it was the Ottoman cavalrymen that decided the outcome. They finally overran their Hungarian opponents and turned their attention to the German infantry. Seeing that his position was hopeless, Hunyadi withdrew. Half his force had died in the battle. The Ottomans had lost about 33,000 men. But Murad had destroyed the Hungarian threat to his territories in the Balkans. He had also seen the effectiveness of gunpowder weapons and ordered that his Janissaries should henceforth be equipped with firearms.

Armies of cavalry

The Ottomans built up a powerful fighting force in their wars in southern Europe. Ottoman armies were invariably large, and most troops were mounted on horses. The vast majority were light, unarmored horsemen equipped with bows or javelins. These could not stand up to Europe's armored heavy cavalry but were much more mobile and maneuverable in battle.

THE SIEGE OF CONSTANTINOPLE

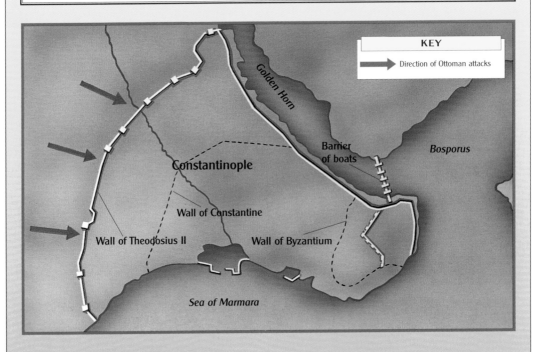

KEY

→ Direction of Ottoman attacks

Golden Horn

Barrier of boats

Bosporus

Constantinople

Wall of Constantine

Wall of Theodosius II

Wall of Byzantium

Sea of Marmara

The siege of Constantinople began in early April 1453. Mehmed II's army numbered about 80,000 men plus 70 heavy cannon, including enormous wall-smashing bombards, commanded by a Christian. The sultan also had a body of miners to dig under the city walls, along with a fleet of perhaps 300 warships.

The 10,000 troops defending the walls of Constantinople fought off the first attacks. They shot down the advancing Ottomans or doused them with Greek fire. The fighting was at close quarters, and the Ottomans suffered great losses. The Byzantines also found the Ottoman miners. They placed poisonous "stinkpots" in the tunnels to gas the Ottomans or blew them up with gunpowder.

On May 29 Mehmed's cannon finally punched a big hole in the city walls. A hand-to-hand battle followed as the Byzantines, including Emperor Constantine XI, tried desperately to keep the Ottomans out. The defenders had so few troops that they had to leave parts of the walls almost unmanned. The Ottomans found one of these weak points and poured in. The defenders were slaughtered almost to a man, including Constantine.

Since they had stormed the city, the Ottomans were allowed to plunder its treasures. Their looting spree lasted for three days. The fall of Constantinople marked the end of the Byzantine Empire. The great city became the capital of the new empire of the Ottomans.

Ottoman infantry, other than the corps of Janissaries, was poorly trained, lightly equipped, and of little use except for chasing a defeated enemy. However, the vast numbers of such infantry often weakened the morale of their enemies.

The end of the Byzantine Empire

In 1451 Murad II died and was succeeded by his son Mehmed II, an equally capable ruler. The Balkans were still not fully under Ottoman rule, but Mehmed wanted to capture Constantinople. It was almost all that was left of the Byzantine Empire. For many years the Ottomans had wanted the great and ancient city as their capital. In April 1453 Mehmed at the head of 80,000 men captured Constantinople after a 50-day siege.

He renamed the captured city Istanbul and made it the new Ottoman capital. Mehmed had destroyed the last remnants of the Byzantine Empire. He went on to bring almost the whole of Greece and the Balkans firmly under Ottoman control before his death. To the east he conquered much of the rest of Anatolia. Later sultans would expand the Ottoman Empire even farther.

The Ottoman Turks begin the final assault on Constantinople on May 29, 1453. The outnumbered Byzantine garrison could not man all of the city's walls, and the Ottomans were therefore able to break through an undefended section.

69

THE NEW PROFESSIONAL ARMIES

During the second half of the 15th century the nature of warfare began to undergo a profound change. The armies of previous centuries, which were dominated by armored knights, began to be replaced by semiprofessional and professional forces in which foot soldiers became increasingly important. These troops were better organized and slowly began to be equipped with gunpowder weapons. Firearms and cannon played an increasingly important role in warfare. These changes were most noticeable in Western Europe.

Three soldiers of Charles the Bold's Burgundian army of the 1470s. They were battle-hardened professionals.

In 1461 Charles VII of France died and was succeeded by his son, Louis XI. Much of France was still under the control of nobles. Louis set about bringing their lands under his direct control. The nobles objected strongly to this idea. One of them, Charles the Bold, was Louis's sworn enemy. Charles, who was duke of Burgundy, was especially determined that the French king should not get hold of his land.

In fact Charles's ambition was to make Burgundy even bigger. He built up a professional army similar to the one Louis XI had. Many of his troops were tough veterans of the Hundred Years War. Kings Charles and Louis of France had, in fact, already created the first professional standing army seen in Europe since the Roman Empire, and the duke of Burgundy followed in their footsteps. A large percentage of his army was English.

Battlefield cooperation

By the early 1470s Burgundy had an army of about 8,000 troops. More than half of this force was cavalry, including armored horsemen and mounted bowmen. The remainder was infantry, which consisted of missilemen (bowmen and handgunners) and soldiers armed with extra-long spears called pikes. Charles divided his troops into units known as companies. Each of these contained a mixture of all these different kinds of cavalry and infantry soldiers. The cavalry and infantry practiced working together so that they could cooperate on the battlefield. To back up his army, Charles had an artillery section, and created a supply train to feed his soldiers.

The siege of Neuss

In 1474 Charles the Bold was given an opportunity to send his new army into action. In the spring the small city of Neuss in what is now Germany rebelled against the archbishop of Cologne. Charles decided to support the archbishop against the rebels. He marched an army plus artillery to Neuss and laid siege to the city. Charles's guns pounded the city's walls to pieces. But his troops could not break in and the siege dragged on.

In the summer of 1475 the German emperor, Frederick II, stepped into the quarrel and led an army to the besieged city's rescue. Charles got word that Frederick had arrived in the area and went straight on the attack. He turned his army on Frederick's forces and opened fire with his artillery. Faced with Charles's powerful army, Frederick decided not to give battle. Instead peace talks took place. Charles agreed to end the siege of Neuss in return for Frederick's help in the future.

Charles the Bold's wars against the Swiss were a disaster for Burgundy. The Swiss had the best army anywhere in Europe at the time.

The Swiss were worried about Charles's attempts to enlarge his territories. To put a stop to Charles's expansion, they laid siege to the Burgundian town of Héricourt in November 1474. When Charles sent an army to Héricourt's rescue on the 13th, the Swiss defeated it. With Charles's army driven off, the Swiss then captured other Burgundian border lands.

The garrison executed

Charles did not respond until early in 1476. But when he did he acted ruthlessly. In February Charles marched into Swiss territory and forced the town of Grandson to surrender. He then hanged all the Swiss troops he could find in the town.

The Swiss wasted no time in sending a force to avenge their dead comrades. On March 2 they arrived at Grandson. Charles had an army of 15,000 men, including archers, heavy cavalry,

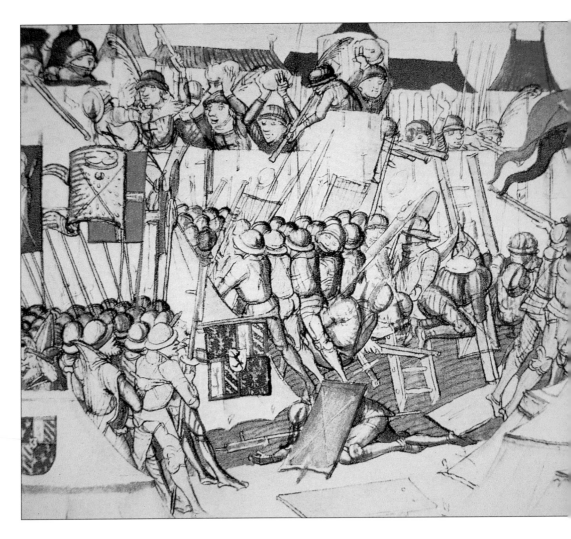

Charles the Bold's Burgundian forces storm the Swiss town of Grandson in February 1476. His victory was soon overturned. On March 2 his army was smashed by a Swiss relief force.

handgunners, and artillery. He formed up outside Grandson, with Lake Neuchâtel on his right. The Swiss infantry force numbered about 18,000 men and was divided into three sections. Each consisted of a dense, tightly packed column of infantry equipped with pikes.

As Charles waited, the first Swiss section came over a hill toward the Burgundians and marched straight into the attack. Charles attacked in turn, sending out two heavy cavalry charges. He also peppered the Swiss with arrows and gunshots. Even so the Swiss kept coming. They were well-known for the speed of their maneuvers on the battlefield. Charles then decided to pull back his center forces and leave his right-hand and left-hand forces in their original position. The Swiss were still marching in a solid block and Charles's aim was to make this block follow his retreating center. Once the Swiss had gone past, the Burgundian forces to the left and right could close in behind them. The Swiss would be surrounded and cut off.

As Charles put his plan into action, the remaining two Swiss sections appeared on the battlefield. The Burgundians on the flanks saw that their center was withdrawing. Unsure of what was going on, they panicked. The whole of Charles's army then started to retreat. The Swiss marched on, cutting down Burgundians wherever they caught up with them. About 1,000 Burgundian troops died at Grandson, along with 200 Swiss. The Swiss captured much of Charles's artillery.

Defeated by the Swiss

Charles did not give up. In June he laid siege to the Swiss village of Morat with a force of 20,000 men. Again he was heavily defeated by a Swiss army coming to the rescue. Still Charles was determined to carry on. That fall the duke of Lorraine, an ally of the Swiss, recaptured Nancy, capital of Lorraine. Charles immediately laid siege to the city even though he could not get supplies to his army. It was a bad mistake. A Swiss army arrived in the depths of winter to support the people of Lorraine.

On January 5, 1477, Charles set out his artillery to block the route he expected the Swiss to take. Part of the Swiss force advanced that way, as expected. But another section marched around the outside of Charles's defenses and launched a surprise attack on the Burgundians from the side. The Burgundian army was caught between the two Swiss forces and destroyed.

Charles was killed in the one-sided battle as he tried to rally his army but his remains were not found until two days later. Wolves had torn his body to pieces, and it was barely recognizable even to

THE BATTLE OF MORAT

In June 1476 Charles the Bold laid siege to the Swiss village of Morat on the shores of Lake Morat. Expecting the Swiss to send an army to its rescue, Charles had his men dig themselves a trench. He also ordered them to drive sharp stakes into the ground behind the trench to make it even more difficult for the Swiss to attack. He then placed his archers and artillery behind these defenses and waited for the Swiss army to arrive.

The Swiss army of 25,000 arrived in the area on June 22. They marched out of sight through the woods until almost the last moment. Suddenly they appeared while most of Charles's army was resting in camp.

The Swiss pikemen and halberdiers (soldiers armed with axes mounted on poles) plowed through the half-empty defenses, slaughtering everyone in their way. One Burgundian force of some 7,000 men was trapped against the lake. The Swiss killed them all. One third of Charles's army of 20,000 died.

THE SWISS WAR MACHINE

In the 15th century the troops of the Swiss federation were among the most feared in the world. They were well trained, highly disciplined, and ruthless. The Swiss forces were made up mostly of infantry with very few cavalry.

The majority were armed with pikes 18 feet (5.5 m) in length capped with metal spearheads. But some carried handguns or crossbows, and others were equipped with halberds or very large swords. A halberd could open up 15th-century armor like a sardine can when it was swung with two hands.

The Swiss infantry marched into battle in two or three blocks of men about 30 soldiers wide and up to 100 deep. The blocks of troops went straight into combat without stopping to form a battle line.

The Swiss pike blocks could halt a charge by the heaviest armored cavalry and they completely terrified their enemies because of their fighting reputation. The Swiss were particularly feared for not taking prisoners.

those who knew him well. Charles's defeat and death at Nancy put an end to Burgundy as an independent state. Louis XI took over most of the dead duke's lands and added them to France.

Charles had had one of the most modern armies of the day. It was highly trained and had good equipment, but he had not used it wisely. The Swiss had outmaneuvered Charles and canceled his advantage. The Swiss had proved themselves the best infantry in Europe and began to hire themselves as mercenaries. The Swiss were so successful that other countries formed similar units.

France fights on

Despite the failures of Charles the Bold's army against the Swiss infantry, it was not the end for full-time professional armies. In the 1490s France showed that such forces were the wave of the future. In 1494 Charles VIII of France attacked Naples in southern Italy. Charles VIII had succeeded his father, Louis XI, in 1483. He claimed that, according to the laws of inheritance that were common at the time, Naples should be part of his kingdom. Charles took control of Naples. But other European powers were worried about what Charles might do next. Several of them, including the Italian states of Milan and Venice, got together to oppose French expansion. This alliance worried Charles VIII. He decided to return to France. Milan and Venice sent an army to ambush Charles as he crossed the Apennine Mountains.

Mercenary armies

For some time Italian cities had used mercenaries. These troops were called condottieri. Over the years the condottieri had gained a bad reputation. They fought for money, and condottieri sometimes changed sides if a noble offered them more money to fight

The death of Charles the Bold (bottom left) at the Battle of Nancy. This great military innovator was unfortunate because he chose to take on the superior Swiss.

for him instead of for his enemy. Because they fought for money, they saw no reason to get hurt in battle if it was not necessary. Some battles between condottieri were no more than maneuvers.

On July 6, 1495, the condottieri of Milan and Venice attacked Charles VIII's French army at Fornovo in northern Italy. The French were expecting this ambush. When the Italian cavalry attacked, Charles's army opened up with its artillery. Then the French cavalry counterattacked. The French took up position, taking advantage of a river that was in flood. They placed their artillery to cover any Italian attack and began bombarding the enemy. The condottieri were probably expecting a typical "bloodless" battle. However, the French had other ideas.

The French attacked ruthlessly, leaving more than 3,000 condottieri dead scattered on the battlefield. Between 100 and 200 of their own troops died. The French had shown what a disciplined, well-trained, and well-led professional army could do in battle. The age of the part-time soldier was coming to an end, and the day of the hardened professional warrior had arrived. Warfare was entering a new era, one in which skill, experience, and training became more important than background and birth.

CONFLICT IN THE FAR EAST

In 1388 the Chinese Ming dynasty overthrew the Mongol Yuan dynasty to take control of China. The turning point was the Chinese victory over the Mongols at the Battle of the Kerulen River in eastern Mongolia and the capture of Karakorum, the Mongol capital. In the early 15th century the Ming were at their most powerful. Japan was beset by civil wars as great warlords struggled to win absolute power over their rivals. By the end of the 15th century both China and Japan were emerging as dominant powers in the Far East.

A Japanese samurai (knight). Warfare in medieval Japan was full of ritual as the samurai fought one another on the basis of a very strict military code of conduct.

Even though the Ming had thrown the Mongols out, these warlike tribesmen were still a threat to northern China. To prevent a Mongol attack the Ming emperor Yung-lo decided to attack first. In 1410 he led an army through the Great Wall and into Mongol territory. He smashed the Mongols at the Onon River in the northeast. Yung-lo marched into Mongolia four more times over the next 14 years. He succeeded in keeping the Mongols out of China. Yung-lo also set about expanding the Ming Empire.

In 1405 a civil war began in Annam, part of what is now Vietnam. To help out the Annamite royal family, Yung-lo sent 200,000 troops, who defeated the opposition forces. Instead of handing the country back to the royal family, however, Yung-lo took control of Annam. The Annamites did not want to be part of China and resisted fiercely. They began a guerrilla war in 1418 and eventually forced the Chinese to leave ten years later.

Naval expeditions

Yung-lo used his navy to extend China's power overseas. From 1405 Yung-lo's admiral Cheng Ho commanded seven large expeditions, sailing right across the Indian Ocean as far as the Arabian Gulf. His first expedition consisted of 26,000 men and 62 ships. Cheng Ho's ships were among the most seaworthy of the day.

During these voyages of exploration Cheng Ho forced a number of rulers to accept Chinese overlordship, including the king of Ceylon (modern Sri Lanka). However, Cheng Ho's voyages came to an end in 1433, and the Chinese gradually lost control of the sea.

In the north, though, the Mongols were becoming strong again. In 1449 the Ming emperor, Ying Tsung, invaded Mongol territory. He was defeated the same year and imprisoned until 1457. The great days of the Ming dynasty were over.

Japan in chaos

To the east, meantime, Japan was being torn apart by civil war. Since the 12th century a military leader called the shogun had ruled Japan. Japan still had an emperor, but he had little power and was little more than a figurehead. Powerful warlords, each with his own kingdom, battled for supreme power Now the shogun had lost control of most of the country, and local nobles ruled their own areas of Japan. With the help of their knights, or samurai, the warring Japanese nobles fought one another to expand their personal territories and power.

One of the many civil wars of the time was the Onin War, which broke out in 1467. The Onin War was fought by some of Japan's strongest families over who was to be the next shogun. Streetfighting between their armies in the Japanese capital, Kyoto, led to the city being burned to the ground. And not only were the nobles at war. In 1465 two groups of Buddhist monks, the Tendai and the Shin, fought one another for power.

The Tendai won by attacking the Shin monastery in Kyoto and burning it to the ground. Japan remained in chaos until the middle of the 16th century, when a single warlord, Ieyasu Tokugawa, gained absolute power by defeating all his rivals and established a ruling dynasty that would last for centuries.

CHENG HO

One of the greatest military explorers of all time, Cheng Ho was a Muslim who was born in China's Yunnan province. He fought with great bravery during the civil war that put Yung-lo on the throne. Between 1405 and 1433 Cheng Ho was ordered to carry out a number of great maritime expeditions.

During his first three voyages his fleet traveled to India and Ceylon (now Sri Lanka). The fifth voyage took Cheng Ho to the Arabian Gulf, and the seventh landed at several points along the East African coast.

For reasons unknown, Cheng Ho was ordered by the emperor to stop his explorations despite the trading possibilities they had opened up.

Cheng Ho died in 1451, and Chinese attempts to develop economic ties with other trading nations effectively died with him. Henceforth, the country was one of the most isolated and inward-looking nations on Earth.

GLOSSARY

bombard An early type of cannon, usually little more than an iron barrel strengthened with thick iron bands. They were slow to load and fire, not very accurate, and liable to burst explosively.

castle A type of fortification, usually built of stone, sited to protect a key point, such as a river crossing or mountain pass. Castles were usually the home of a local lord, his family, and followers.

chain mail A type of flexible armor consisting of interlinked metal rings. It could cover the entire body or just a vulnerable part, such as the head.

gunpowder An explosive made by combining quantities of saltpeter, sulfur, and charcoal. It was probably developed by the Chinese in the 9th century, but was first used regularly in warfare in Europe from the mid-14th century.

handgun In warfare, an early type of firearm consisting of a heavy barrel mounted on a wooden stock. Not very accurate, handguns were also heavy, prone to misfiring, and had a short range.

heraldry A means of identification worn by medieval lords and knights on their clothes and shields. A combination of colors, geometrical shapes, animals, mythical beasts, and other objects identified the particular lord and his family. Simplified devices were often worn by retainers as a means of identifying their allegiance.

knight The best trained and equipped soldier of the Middle Ages, generally from a noble family. Knights wore armor and usually fought on horseback. Their chief tactic was a thunderous charge. Weapons included a lance, sword, or ax.

longboat A Viking warship. Powered by oars and a single sail, these wooden vessels were extremely seaworthy and could sail the shallowest waters because of their shallow draft.

man-at-arms A medieval professional soldier who was usually a retainer of a lord or knight. Typical weapons included a sword, spear, dagger, longbow, or crossbow.

plate armor A type of protective armor consisting of a number of metal sheets shaped to follow the contour of the human body. By the 14th century expensive suits of armor covered knights from head to foot.

BIBLIOGRAPHY

Note: *An asterisk (*) denotes a Young Adult title.*

Bartusis, Mark C. *The Late Byzantine Army: Arms and Society 1204–1453.* University of Pennsylvania Press, 1997

*Brownstone, David and Franck, Irene. *Timelines of Warfare From 100,000 B.C. to the Present.* Little, Brown and Company, 1994

*Byam, Michelle. *Arms and Armor.* Eyewitness Books, 1988

DeVries, Kelly. *Infantry Warfare in the Early Fourteenth Century.* Boydell and Brewer, Inc., 1998

*Dijkstra, Henk, ed. *History of the Ancient and Medieval World.* Marshall Cavendish, 1996

Dupuy, R. Ernest and Dupuy, Trevor. *The Collins Encyclopedia of Military History.* HarperCollins, 1993

Dupuy, R.E., Johnson, Curt, and Bongard, David L. *The Harper Encyclopedia of Military Biography.* HarperCollins, 1995

*Lace, William W. *The Battle of Hastings: Battles of the Middle Ages.* Lucent Books, 1996

Matthews, John and Stewart, Bob. *Warriors of Medieval Times.* Sterling Publishing, 1993

Sawyer, Peter (editor). *The Oxford Illustrated History of the Vikings.* Oxford University Press, Inc, 1997

Sire, H.J.A. *The Knights of Malta.* Yale University Press, 1996

Verbruggen, J.F. *The Art of Warfare in Western Europe During the Middle Ages.* Boydell and Brewer, Inc., 1997

*Warner, Philip. *Sieges of the Middle Ages.* Barnes and Noble, 1994

INDEX

ACKNOWLEDGMENTS

Cover (main picture) Peter Newark's Military Pictures, (inset) AKG Photo, London; page 1 AKG Photo, London; page 5 AKG Photo, London; page 6 AKG Photo, London; page 7 Hulton Getty Collection; page 10 AKG Photo, London; page 13 AKG Photo, London; page 14 AKG Photo, London; page 16 AKG Photo, London; page 18 Hulton Getty Collection; page 21 AKG Photo, London; page 22 The Bridgeman Art Library; page 25 AKG Photo, London; page 26 AKG Photo, London/Erich Lessing; page 27 AKG Photo, London; page 29 Hulton Getty Collection; pages 30 and 31 Hulton Getty Collection; page 32 AKG Photo, London; page 34 AKG Photo, London; page 36 AKG Photo, London; page 37 Hulton Getty Collection; page 38 AKG Photo, London; page 40 Hulton Getty Collection; page 41 Hulton Getty Collection; page 42 Peter Newark's Historical Pictures; page 43 Peter Newark's Military Pictures; page 45 Peter Newark's Historical Pictures; page 47 Mary Evans Picture Library; page 48 AKG Photo, London; page 50 AKG Photo, London; page 52 Hulton Getty Collection; page 55 Hulton Getty Collection; page 57 Hulton Getty Collection; page 58 Hulton Getty Collection; page 59 AKG Photo, London; page 61 AKG Photo, London; page 63 Peter Newark's Military Pictures; page 64 Peter Newark's Military Pictures; page 66 Peter Newark's Military Pictures; page 69 Peter Newark's Historical Pictures; page 70 Peter Newark's Historical Pictures; page 72 Peter Newark's Military Pictures; page 75 AKG Photo, London; page 76 AKG Photo, London.

5 9/01